NOWHERE ELSE IN THE WORLD

NOWHERE ELSE IN THE WORLD

Nicholas Brash
Jane Gleeson-White

HUTCHINSON AUSTRALIA

COVER:
Mystery Bay is on the south coast of New South
Wales near Narooma in the Eurobodalla Shire,
which is a region of fishing villages and forests,
resort towns and cheese factories, famous for its
cheeses and record tuna, kingfish and
shark catches.

Century Hutchinson Australia Pty Ltd
89–91 Albion Street, Surry Hills, New South Wales, 2010

Sydney London Auckland
Johannesburg and agencies throughout the world

First published in 1989
in association with Bow Press
Bow Publications Pty Limited
208 Victoria Road, Drummoyne, New South Wales, 2047

Distributed by Century Hutchinson Australia Pty Ltd

Text copyright © Nicholas Brash

National Library of Australia
Cataloguing-in-Publication data

Brash, Nicholas, 1946–
   Australia, nowhere else in the world.

   ISBN 0 09 169520 1.

   1. Australia — Description and travel — 1976–   .2.
   Australia — Social life and customs — 1976–   .I.
   Gleeson-White, Jane II. Title

994.06'3

Designed by Bruno Jean Grasswill
Typeset by Love Computer Typesetting
Production by Vantage Graphics
Printed in Singapore by Tien Wah

CONTENTS

INTRODUCTION

The world shrinks a little every day; jets sweep more people into more countries, newspapers span the world, television networks pry open new doors in new lands. But mass marketing, mass travel, mass information will never globalise *feelings*.

And Australia is like Nowhere Else In The World. There is a feeling that cannot be labelled English, or American, or European or Asian. There is an elusive scent in the air that vanishes as you almost pinpoint it, colours that affront with their boldness or enchant with their changing moods, flowers too unusual to be accepted and animals too unlikely to be believed.

The vastness is immeasurable and almost frightening. The outback of Australia is a blistered land with no clear sense of time and distance. A humbling environment. Sitting alone in the Outback is like bobbing in a dinghy in the middle of the Pacific Ocean. There's cruelty in the world of Australia: the sadness after a bushfire, blackened earth supporting a few spindly trunks. Or the decline of a cliff slowly being eroded by an inexorable ocean.

But there's delight: the wonder on a country boy's face as he sees the ocean for the first time; the sleepy eyes of a koala sitting looking curiously at the world from the limb of a gum in the early morning light as he looks for a fork to sleep in.

There are no cathedrals steeped in 400 or 500 years of history. But there are caves where long before cathedrals were envisioned, Australian aboriginals were celebrating their own spirituality.

These are the feelings that make Australia unique. Purists will look at, say, the ghost gum and the knowledgeable may comment that it is also found in Papua New Guinea. Trees, like birds, migrate very easily, their spore carried on the winds. But the ghost gum is essentially Australian. It is part of the feeling. Similarly, other countries have harbours, or Opera Houses, or Bridges, or sports grounds. But Sydney Harbour and the MCG are essentially Australian; they are part of the land that is like Nowhere Else In The World.

LANDMARKS

Nature created the body of Australia; man has added a few tiny accessories. Sometimes they've enhanced the naked body, occasionally they've soured the sweetness of form and content. But even the raw touches cannot detract from the majesty of the island continent. And when man adds his own touches they can sometimes enhance superbly: Utzon's visionary Opera House gave Sydney Harbour a final touch, the fireworks displays which lit up the Harbour and the Opera House throughout the Bicentennial Year gave nature a helping hand. When the city of Melbourne approved the MCG it created one of the great sports arenas in the world. But in the main, man has placed only a few tiny dots of paint on nature's Promethean canvas.

Ayers Rock, Uluru in the Aboriginal, is the odd symbol of Australia. Odd because so many of Australia's inhabitants live on the seaboard, for them the beach and the surf *are* Australia. But Ayers Rock is the true representative of the island continent. It is alone, it is vast, it is formidable.

Ayers Rock juts out of the flat, seemingly barren landscape changing colours throughout the day, moody and vaguely menacing. Ayers Rock is the heart of the country. It stands there challenging and patient, the symbol of a vast and timeless continent. For 300 million years the Rock has watched the moods and changes of Australia: mountains have come and gone, inland seas have flooded and dried, deserts have crept in with their sandshoes tucked under their arms. In the height of the day with the dry sky an intense blue Uluru is a burnt umber with a trace of orange, a pigment da Vinci would have seized on with glee. But dusk brings the mood swings of the Rock; waves of blue and purple and a nightstalker black cross the Rock. Tourists standing chattering happily minutes before are silenced by the majesty of the moment, their talk replaced by the clicking and flashdance of cameras.

The Rock is the unconquerable symbol of Australia; Chambers Pillar is its frailer little brother. The Pillar is a time-eaten monolith surrounded by sandy, stony plains. If the Rock reflects the power of the Australian environment, the Pillar reveals the harshness. Drought and dust storms are part of Australia's natural cycle. When the drought dries the land to dust the inevitable winds will sweep away tonnes of soil, leaving a barren land for the next generation to rebuild. Australia is a land for patient people.

And it is a big land, the globe's largest island though smallest continent. The Red Centre is almost two million square kilometres of badlands with its four great deserts. But if the Outback seems vast, the coastline is even more imposing. The largest coral reef in the world, the Great Barrier Reef, runs for 2300km along the continental shelf of northeastern Australia. Ironically, the 'deserts' are still in attendance; the tropical currents have lost most of their marine richness when they wash the outer edge of the reef. Instead they contain an abundance of calcium carbonate, the raw material the chains of coral convert to living rock. The Reef is comprised of more than 350 species of coral — more than one-third of the world's 1000 species — all fighting for sunlight, the primary force for growth.

And if the deserts of the Outback are found in a different form off the coast so too is the harshness. Some species of fish feed on the coral, man can wreak havoc with mineral exploitation or over-tourism and there is always the Crown of Thorns, a species of sea star and a prodigious predator which turns its stomach inside out to suck the life out of a coral colony.

The Great Barrier Reef is one of the great natural wonders of the world. It is complemented by the Australian coastline: beaches and cliffs, bays and estuaries. A playground for millionaires and unemployed alike. This is the zone where the poor can enjoy the leisure life of the megarich . . . and that must be like nowhere else in the world! Swimming costumes are the great leveller. A paunch fuelled by Moet & Chandon is no different than that plumped by keg beer. The beaches sculpted by nature in golden hues are crowded by people in rainbows of costumes. But there are bays with dark black-green water curling around the roots of mangroves where only a leathery brown fisherman sits in an old aluminium tender — half-hoping he doesn't catch a fish to disrupt his daydream.

The 15,997 nautical miles of coastline are a series of myriad landmarks in themselves, some minute, some dominant such as the Twelve Apostles. Some are remote, like Mystery Bay on New South Wales' South Coast, featured on the cover. An eerie moonscape with morning fog hovering over the stark black rocks and the flawless sand left smooth by the receding tide.

There are beaches such as Pebbly Beach, barely three hours drive from a city of four million, where wallabies bob nonchalantly on to the sand at sunrise, unperturbed by the handful of campers blearily climbing out of their tents.

The coastline is a series of vastly different panoramas: The Nullarbor Plain comes to an abrupt halt at the Great Southern Ocean, plunging into the water; the coast of Tasmania features a series of stark cruel cliffs seeming to fight to hold

The spectacular granite boulders of Wilson's Promontory, the southernmost point of the Australian continent and one of Australia's loveliest and most popular national parks. It is a landscape of grey granite headlands, rugged mountains and foaming seas. Wilson's Promontory was named by Governor Hunter in 1798, on the recommendation of George Bass and Matthew Flinders, after Thomas Wilson, a London merchant who provided Bass and Flinders with the supplies for their journeys. The beautiful coastline, white beaches and dramatic rocky slopes and headlands of Wilson's Promontory attract over half a million visitors a year. Koalas, wombats, possums, emus and kangaroos live happily in the peaceful bush of Wilson's Promontory.

their footing as the ocean batters them; in Western Australia's north, tidal drops as high as 12m have carved wrinkles in the face of the land.

At Byron Bay, near the New South Wales/Queensland border, Cape Byron juts out proudly into the Pacific; this is the easternmost point of Australia, the first land to catch the rising sun. On the northern side of the Cape is the gold and cream face of Australia: a beach where the waves roll in and the tension rolls away. This is beachland Australia at its near best. Not perfection; that lies closer to urban Australia: at Pearl Beach, a scant hour's drive from Sydney. An image beach, too impeccable to be real. In front of the beach lies Lion Rock, guarding the entrance to the mighty Hawkesbury waterway and the sheltered boating playground of Pittwater. The Pacific falls in here, rather than rolling in. Lapping gently on a golden mixture of fine sand and the delicate shell. A handful of houses stand on the beachfront, nothing garish, nothing over-the-top. Just old-fashioned summer houses — at modern prices.

But the natural landmarks of Australia are more than just badlands and coastlines. More than desert monoliths and coral reefs. There are graceful waterfalls that fall like silver tears down a face of black granite, shimmering and glistening in the light filtering through a rainforest canopy. Or sand dunes of purple and cream which fold like satin sheets, puckering and turning on a desert bed.

This is an enormous land, where seasons and time zones change. Australia, statistically, is 7,682,300 sq km or on a comparable scale with other parts of the world, nearly 14 times bigger than France or 58 times bigger than England. You could fit 25 Italies into the borders of mainland Australia. And the island State, Tasmania, is bigger than Switzerland. The Great Dividing Range which runs parallel with the East Coast for 2000km is tropical at its northern end and sub-alpine at the southern extremity. Mount Kosciukso is the highest point in the island continent at 2228m; the lowest point is Lake Eyre, 16m below sea level.

Statistics are fascinating. But they don't give you the feel of Australia. They can't conjure up the smell of a still mangrove swamp in the East Alligator River or the salty taste of the clear water in a Whitsunday Passage lagoon. Statistics can't tell you that the sunset over Tennant Creek will stop your breath and slow your heartbeat until you seem part of the slow still landscape. Or create the sound of a Tasmanian rainforest tap . . . as last night's rain drips slowly from the branch of a southern beech into an unseen rockpool. The rainforests of the south are simple-beech, firs, ferns. But in the tropical north they flourish with an abundance and variety. At first glance they seem like any tropical rainforest, like Malaya or Brazil. There's little ostensible evidence they are like nowhere else in the world. Many of the world's most ancient flowering plants exist only in the rainforests of northern Queensland. There are more than 1200 different species of trees and higher plants in these rainforests, all fighting for sunlight. And if the rainforests are still and cool at their base, the action is going on high in the canopy. Possums rule this rooftop world. They evolved in rainforests and the earliest species still live there. The dim, almost mysterious world of the rainforest will end abruptly, giving way to the eucalypt forests which almost invariably are neighbours. The eucalypt is the more recognisable face of the Australian bush, helped by its charm-filled resident, the koala, which prefers the leaves of red gums in the northern woodlands and grey gums in the southeast.

Heathlands, alps, fiords, white water rapids and barely moving rivers,

Australia is a diversity of landmarks. And off the mainland are the islands, landmarks in their own right. Some are bare, bleak guardians with only a remote lighthouse as a marker, others are tropical oases.

The natural landmarks of Australia are many and various. The manmade landmarks are fewer but as diverse. They encompass the beautiful (the Sydney Opera House, the Arts Centre of Victoria), the unusual (the 'Superman' Building, Parliament), the bold (Darling Harbour, Centrepoint), the controversial (the Monorail, the Croc Hotel) and the garish (the Big Banana and the Big Pineapple).

The Coathanger, Sydney's Harbour Bridge, since its completion nearly 60 years ago, has been the symbol of European arrival in Australia. But the Bridge is rapidly being surpassed by its neighbour, virtually nestling at its feet: the Sydney Opera House. It has its detractors but visitors and residents alike hold it in awe. Summer's morning light paints it a delicate daffodil gold, a thin winter sunshine turns it pearly silver, the setting sun turns its city-facing sails a soft pink: like Ayers Rock, the Opera House is a moody building changing with the light and the seasons. Harbour hydrofoils cut close to the corner of the masterpiece, their spray splashing on the rocky base; older, more sedate ferries glide past in respect. The Opera House has become the centrepiece of the most perfect harbour setting in the world.

And Darling Harbour, tucked around the corner, has become the showpiece. Sydney's answer to Fishermen's Wharf in San Francisco, Darling Harbour is an unabashed commercial enterprise. A shopping attraction, a tourist drawcard, a manmade modern money mover. But for all that, it has style. Cities in other parts of the world have approached the designers to recreate similar centres in places as different from Sydney as Birmingham and Manchester. The centre has oomph. It lives and breathes and sparkles in the water setting. It promises to entertain you.

As entertaining, though not by design, is the show at Australia's newest and costliest building: Parliament House in Canberra. Opened on May 9, 1988 by Queen Elizabeth, Parliament House's current estimated finished cost is $1.1billion. Elected politicians live a high profile life; but in Coober Pedy the opal miners elect to live underground. On the fringe of the huge Woomera Prohibited Area where Australia and England held atomic tests in the 1950s, Coober Pedy is the world's largest opal-producing centre. A barren, apocalyptic area where most of the inhabitants live in former shafts beneath the desert. In the cool of their underground apartments, carved out to surprising comfort and occasionally, luxury, they escape the 50°C heat (122°F). There is even an underground chapel for cool comfort.

Not all the artificial landmarks are as permanent. Moomba, the Sydney Harbour Fireworks and the Melbourne Cup are ephemeral drawcards. Sydney has the setting but Melbourne has the events. Moomba is an aboriginal word meaning 'let's get together and have fun'. It's Mardi Gras time in what is normally a more conservative Melbourne. Waterskiers cut swathes through the impassive Yarra River, while food and wine tastings, carnivals and music festivals build up the tempo to the climactic parade of floats through the city. Moomba is essentially a Melbourne festival but the Melbourne Cup belongs to the nation, although some may say, cynically, it belongs to New Zealand whose racehorses have dominated the event, certainly in the post-war era. On the first Tuesday of November for the 3min 20sec it takes to run the 3200m, Australia comes together. Fortunes come

The wattle is Australia's national floral emblem and its colours can be found in the green and gold of the Australian sports uniforms. Wattles belong to the genus Acacia — Australian acacias are the most decorative of the acacias and burst into swathes of golden blossom in winter and spring. The flowers have no petals, only stamens, but develop into long pods like peas. This oleander wattle (Acacia neriifolia) may be a tall shrub or a tree, growing to 10m and is found in New South Wales and Queensland.

and go, battlers from the bush stand alongside the nation's richest men and office staff cheer along with managing director in the office sweep. This is the sporting event that became a national landmark.

Sydney Harbour fireworks displays will never stop the country but for their own brief lifespan they bring a colour and excitement that is unique. The Bicentennial Year was an over-the-top extravaganza with the Japanese, the Navy, the City and Perth brewer Alan Bond all turning on a 'night to remember'. Flash in the pan, they may be, but the fireworks on the harbour nights draw the oohs and aahs.

The pubs of Australia, from the earliest in The Rocks of Sydney, to the outback or the 1889 quaintness of Brisbane's Breakfast Creek Hotel are micro-landmarks. Certainly to locals who will often meet at The Pub, or the Albert or The Star as the case may be.

The Rocks is the birthplace of European Australia. The colony of New South Wales sprang up on its little humps and ridges. Razor gangs and madams clashed with the constabulary in those early days. Today it is a major restoration showpiece with old wool sheds, bond stores and warehouses converted to opal centres, art galleries and houses selling Australiana. But in the cobblestone alleyways and between the tarted-up stone walls lies the images of the past.

The Rocks and the natural beauty of Sydney Harbour have found harmony. But man is not always as benevolent with nature: in a desperate drive to prove the biggest island in the world can outTexas Texas Australians have built some garish monuments: giant pineapples, enormous cows, marlin, trout, wine bottles, lobsters, oranges, merino, crocodiles . . . all larger than life. The pineapple at Gympie, north of Brisbane is 16m high and 7.6m in diameter. Yandina's giant cow is 8m high and nearly 11m long; Cairns boasts a 20m high black marlin and Adaminaby a 12m trout. There's a 17m wine bottle at Griffith and a giant merino ram at Campbell Town, Tasmania. Bunyips, cassowaries, penguins, buffalo, even Ned Kelly: They are all featured in gigantic form but in reality are tiny blemishes on a remarkable face.

Far from such momentary aberrations are the National Parks of Australia, foremost among them Kakadu in the Northern Territory, described by UNESCO in 1981 as one of the world's last great natural reserves. The 20,000sq km of the park sprawls across marshes creeks and floodplains of the East and South Alligator rivers. The dry season, from April to October or even November sees the wildlife concentrated on the few waterholes before the big wet. Kakadu is home to more than one-third of the birds of Australia, fifty fish species live in the waters including the prized gamefish, the barramundi. They share the park with wallaroos, rock wallabies, the northern quoll, pythons, geckos, a variety of bats. But the daddy of them all, the big attraction at Kakadu is the saltwater crocodile. They are one of the few animals to stalk humans calculatedly, floating with only their nostrils and eyes showing. Far from Kakadu, in Tasmania, is a national park of a very different nature: Cradle Mountain and Lake St Clair, which embraces a wide expanse of subalpine and alpine moorlands. Cradle Mountain, in the north of the park is a Tasmanian landmark with its 1545m peak a magnet for storms. Kakadu and Cradle Mountain, two of the very different landmarks and faces of Australia.

The celebration of two hundred years of European settlement in Australia was marked by the Parade of Sail of seventeen tall ships on Australia Day. The ships came from all over the world to moor at Darling Harbour and to flaunt their beautiful masts and sails across the harbour on January 26. The ship most similar to those of the First Fleet was the replica *Bounty*, which re-enacted the voyage of the First Fleet. The other ships in the re-enactment were more modern and included four brigantines:

the *Soren Larsen* from England, the *R. Tucker Thompson* from New Zealand, the *Marie Galante* and *Atlantic Clipper* from Australia, and the Canadian barquentine *Svanen*. The Bicentennial fleet was led by *Gorch Foch* and included the fully-rigged Polish ship *Dar Mlodziezy*, the four-masted Spanish barque *Juan de Elcano Sebastian*, the Indian brig *Varuna*, the American barque, *Eagle* and a brand new sail training barquentine, a gift from Britain to the Royal Australian Navy.

Ayers Rock lies 478km south west of Alice Springs and rises 348m above the surrounding plain of red sand and spinifex. 'The Rock' is famous for its dramatic and mysterious beauty — William Christie Gosse, who climbed the north-west face of the Rock in 1873, wrote that the Rock was 'certainly the most wonderful natural feature I have ever seen'. Gosse named the rock after the then premier of South Australia, Sir Henry Ayer, but the two Aboriginal tribes who lived in the area called the Rock, 'Uluru'. The surface of the Rock is intricately patterned with gullies, crevices, fluted ridges and pockmarked with caves. Its soft flaky surface is the result of a weathering process known as exfoliation, caused by the extreme temperature changes of desert climates. The base of Uluru is decorated with rock paintings which depict the Dreamtime legends and lives of the Aboriginal people of the area.

The Melbourne Cricket Ground is one of Australia's most popular sports arenas. It was completed in 1853 and staged its first international cricket match in 1862. The first Test match between Australia and England was also held here, with Australia winning narrowly. The MCG is also the home of Australian Football and each year the Victorian Football League holds its grand final here.

Russell Falls is the most spectacular of the three large waterfalls in Mt Field National Park, Tasmania. The falls are two-tiered, which adds to their beauty — the water cascades 15m over a sheer sandstone cliff before tumbling a second time another 30m into a green valley of tree ferns. Russell Falls is in the Derwent Valley, a land of

emerald green mosses, ferns, giant 60m alpine and
mountain ash, eucalypts, and Tasmanian myrtle, a
uniquely Australian temperate rainforest. The
17,000ha park has been a nature reserve since 1885
and was named after a judge of the Supreme Court
of New South Wales, Judge Barron Field.

23

The spectacular new Darling Harbour centre in Sydney contains a convention centre, an exhibition centre, a maritime museum, the Powerhouse Museum of Science and Technology as well as a superb shopping complex. Part of the Darling Harbour project was the restoration of the Pyrmont Bridge. This swinging bridge used to open to let nineteenth century coal burning freighters into the inner commercial harbour of Sydney and it now

opens again to welcome such floating attractions as the Tall Ships that visited Sydney for its Bicentennial celebrations. The seven storey convention centre at Darling Harbour is the largest convention centre in Australia, catering for 3500 people. The monorail was built to link the new complex at Darling Harbour with the city, and after its much protested beginnings it has become a part of the Sydney skyline.

25

St Andrew's Cathedral and Carringbush Tower (the 'Superman' Building) make a dramatic contrast of style on Sydney's skyline. St Andrew's Cathedral has a long and chequered history, being originally conceived by Governor Macquarie in 1812, but not opened until St Andrew's Day, 1868. The gothic style was eventually adopted for St Andrew's Cathedral in 1846 by the architect Edmund Thomas Blackett. The Carringbush Tower, a futuristic tower of glass topped by a New York deco spire, strangely echoes the gothic steeples of St Andrews. The hexagonal building was completed in 1988 and is covered by a unique blue 'pin-stripe' glass that dominated the greys and silvers of Sydney's other skyscrapers. The forty-three levels of Carringbush Tower begin in a sculptured pavillion at street level which provides a luxurious restaurant and shopping centre. The facade of the pavillion, the foyer and lower floors are composed of nearly 500 tonnes of rare pink, blue and black granite.

The monorail — born to a storm of protest in Sydney — is gradually becoming better accepted. The monorail connects the central business district with the booming Darling Harbour complex.

On 26 January 1988 Sydney celebrated two hundred years of European settlement in Australia with a lavish display of harbourside entertainment, from the re-enactment of the First Fleet landing, to a parade of sail of tall ships culminating in a dramatic explosion of fireworks in the evening. Two million people gathered around the foreshores of the harbour and took to the water in about 10,000 boats. The official celebrations opened at 11.00am at the Opera House with parades of the armed services, music and speeches. At 9.00pm a 200-gun salute triggered a fantastic display of fireworks which showered through the air above Sydney Harbour. Three fireworks barges let off fireworks east and west of the bridge, but the climax of the evening came when 200 jets of light shot up from the Harbour Bridge like candles to celebrate Australia's birthday.

The spectacular rock formations that line the coast of the Port Campbell National Park are the result of 10-20 million years of erosion. The wild Southern Ocean has worn away the soft limestone cliffs to leave such natural features as the group of rock stacks known as the Twelve Apostles, the natural arch of London Bridge and other rock platforms. London Bridge is a double natural archway which is home to a small colony of fairy penguins. The Twelve Apostles are a group of impressive rock stacks that hug the coastline and make up one of Victoria's most famous landmarks.

Two of the Twelve Apostles, lonely sentinels of the
Port Campbell National Park.

Orange, yellow and cream waves of sand dominate the landscape at Eucla, a town on the Eyre Highway which straddles the Nullarbor Plain, linking Western Australia and South Australia. Eucla is just inside the Western Australian border, near the remnants of an old telegraph station that is now almost totally consumed by sand dunes. The telegraph line was once a link between eastern and western Australia, but it was abandoned when an inland line was built along the trans-Australian railway. The main repeater station was at Eucla, which became a busy settlement with a bustling port — the population peaked at ninety. Plagues of rabbits have since eaten the vegetation from the coastal dunes, which has loosened the sand — winds have blown the sandhills inland at a rate of about 25 metres a year and the old town of Eucla is now engulfed in sand.

The Big Merino is a symbol of Goulburn's long association with the Australian sheep industry. Goulburn is about 200km southwest of Sydney and lies in the heart of a rich rural district famous for its wool. The merino is a hardy sheep, introduced to Australia in the early days because of its ability to survive in low rainfall areas. The development of the first 150 years of European settlement in Australia is essentially the story of the Australian wool industry, for it was the demand for grazing land for wool that spurred the exploration and settlement of Australia.

Yet another of the B-I-G symbols which allegedly attract tourists. The Big Crocodile at Adelaide River, in the Northern Territory.

The enormous concrete banana at Coffs Harbour is a symbol of the banana plantations that surround the town. Inside the Big Banana is a Visitors' Centre which displays the various stages and processes involved in the production and sale of bananas. Coffs Harbour is a popular tourist centre on the northern coast of New South Wales, lying where the Great Dividing Range meets the coast.

The Big Pineapple at Sunshine Plantation, 115km north of Brisbane. It is 16m high and contains a Polynesian restaurant, a tropical market and an observation deck from which visitors can look out over the surrounding pineapple plantations.

Cape Byron is the easternmost point of Australia, the first landmark on the continent to see the sunrise. The cape was named by Captain Cook in 1770. The gracious lighthouse of Cape Byron was opened in 1901. It stands on a cliff that looms 90m above the Pacific Ocean, so it does not need a tall tower. The gas light was replaced with an electric light in 1959, giving the lighthouse a power of 2.2 million candelas.

South of Brisbane is the 32km stretch of rolling breakers and golden sands known fittingly as the Gold Coast. This is one of Australia's major tourist areas, with its abundant supply of sunshine, surf lush National Parks, entertainment and excitement. The buildings of Surfers Paradise can be seen in the distance, silhouetted in the dusk as the town prepares for another onslaught of nightime revelry.

Sydney Harbour is synonymous with Sydney itself and is home to Sydney's two most famous manmade landmarks: the Opera House and the Harbour Bridge. One of the most beautiful harbours in the world, Sydney Harbour provides Sydneysiders with entertainment in all forms, from harbourside parks and restaurants, sailing,

swimming and fishing, to a venue for spectacular fireworks displays. Popular with both locals and visitors, Sydney Harbour has also been a popular subject for Australian painters, inspiring some of our greatest artists including Conrad Martens, Arthur Streeton, Lloyd Rees and Brett Whiteley.

The beautiful crescent shape of Lord Howe Island lies north east of Sydney on the southernmost coral reef of the Pacific Ocean. The island is on the World Heritage list, in acknowledgement of its rich cultural past and its valuable natural heritage. Henry Lidgbird Bell discovered Lord Howe Island and one of its two gracious mountain peaks, Mt Lidgbird, is named after him. The island was used to grow kentia palms for export, and was a supply centre for whaling ships. Kentia palms are now the island's second biggest industry.

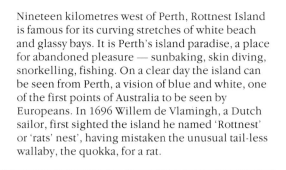

Nineteen kilometres west of Perth, Rottnest Island is famous for its curving stretches of white beach and glassy bays. It is Perth's island paradise, a place for abandoned pleasure — sunbaking, skin diving, snorkelling, fishing. On a clear day the island can be seen from Perth, a vision of blue and white, one of the first points of Australia to be seen by Europeans. In 1696 Willem de Vlamingh, a Dutch sailor, first sighted the island he named 'Rottnest' or 'rats' nest', having mistaken the unusual tail-less wallaby, the quokka, for a rat.

The white spray of the Southern Ocean pounds the shores of Kangaroo Island, Australia's second largest island, not including Tasmania. Kangaroo Island lies off the coast of South Australia and was named by Matthew Flinders when he landed there in 1802. The sculptured limestone cliffs of the island contain many unusual natural features, such as Admiral's Arch at Cape du Couedic. This was once a limestone cave, but the powerful swell of the Southern Ocean has eroded the cave wall so it is now a tunnel with an opening both to the east and west. First settled by convicts from Tasmania, Kangaroo Island later became a whaling station and the centre of rich trapping and sealing industries. Today the island is a wildlife haven — Flinders Chase National Park on its western end is an untouched wilderness with an abundance of animal life.

The new Parliament House in Canberrra was
opened officially in Australia's bicentennial year,
eight years after the winning design was selected.
The new building is carefully integrated into its
surroundings — its central roof is gently curved
and topped with a grassy walkway to recall the
original hilltop of Capitol Hill, on which it is built.
The basic structural form of the building is
provided by two 460m curved granite walls, which
extend along a north-south axis. To the east of the
walls is the chamber of the House of
Representatives and their offices, and to the west is
the Senate Chamber — each chamber retains its
traditional colours, green for the House of
Representatives and red for the Senate. The flag
mast rises 81m above the roof of the building, an
eloquent symbol of Australia's nationhood
toppped by a 12 x 6m national flag. The Forecourt,
Great Verandah and Foyer are open to the public
and decorated with a variety of Australian stone,
timber and specially created Australian art
and crafts.

The AMP building and the neighbouring Comalco
Building dominate the skyline above the Brisbane
River. Brisbane is Australia's third largest city, yet
the sunshine and blue skies make Brisbane a very
easy-going city. Nearly half the population of
Queensland lives in Brisbane's greater
metropolitan area. Brisbane began as a convict
settlement in 1824, when the first convicts arrived.

The red granite forms of Castle Hill make a distinctive backdrop to Townsville, northern Queensland's major city and port, and Queensland's second largest city. Townsville is an easy-going and relaxed tropical city on the edge of a picturesque harbour. Cleveland Bay, Townsville's port, is a major centre for the transport of minerals, sugar and meat, making Townsville a key city for Queensland's industrial sector. Robert Towns, a Sydney businessman, financed the first settlement in this area in 1864, and the town that grew up was named after him.

When night falls, the glowing silhouette of the Wrest Point Federal Hotel-Casino dominates the skyline of Hobart, drawing hundreds of visitors to its tables. Wrest Point, Australia's first Casino, is positioned on a promontory between the Derwent River and Sandy Bay, backed by the towering Beauty of Mt Wellington.

In Kalgoorlie a golden sun sets over the Hainault
Gold Mine, now a tourist attraction where visitors
can go underground to see the workings of a
subterranean gold mine. In June 1893, gold was
discovered in Kalgoorlie in an area so rich with the
metal that it became known as the Golden Mile.
Kalgoorlie, in a riverless semi-desert, is Australia's
richest gold field, and here the gold-struck
fossickers came to live in shacks made of hessian,
kerosene tins and old packing cases while they
searched for their dream.

Ten days of music and cultural activities, fireworks and water skiing culminate in Australia's most spectacular street parade, the Moomba Festival. Held every March, the festival signals the time for Melbourne to take to the streets to dance, to watch the street processions and to join in the festivities. Through the colourful flowerings of fireworks, the elegant spire of the Victorian Arts Centre can be seen. Beside the Yarra River and St Kilda Road, the Arts Centre contains the National Gallery of Victoria, the Melbourne Concert Hall, the Theatres Building, a Performing Arts Museum and a series of restaurants.

JS PAGE:
stness of the Pilbara . . . where giant
hery is dwarfed.

Brisbane joined the world trade stage in 1988 with
the twenty-third World Exposition held here in the
great pavilions and under sails of green and gold.
From 30 April to 30 October, 1988 the $600 million
extravanganza raged on the banks of the Brisbane
River. This was the first Expo held in the southern
hemisphere since 1888, when it was held in
Melbourne to celebrate Australia's centenary. The
theme of 'Expo '88' was 'Leisure in the Age of
Technology', and it collected together the cultural
and technological achievements of thirty-six
nations, fifty-two governments and twenty-five
corporations. A staggering 25,000 performances
were presented to the visitors, performances which
ranged from street artists and buskers to
international singers. Over 175 sculptures were
built for the site of Expo and every day ended with
the light and colour of the fireworks display.

The mighty Murray River is Australia's most important river. It slowly meanders across 2570km of the flat Australian continent, from its source in the Snowy Mountains to its mouth on the Great Southern Ocean. In the past the Murray was a major transport route for the paddlesteamers of the nineteenth century. Today the Murray is a popular recreational river, where people come to relax, to fish or simply to enjoy its breathtaking beauty. Towering red cliffs and gums line much of the gracious river. Waterbirds, such as this efficient fisher, the pelican, are a common sight along the banks and waters of the Murray.

The jagged ridges of Cradle Mountain dominate
the horizon of the Cradle Mountain/Lake St Clair
National Park, Tasmania. Cradle Mountain is a peak
of dolerite that was sculpted in the last Ice Age
15,000 years ago — its cold and misty beauty
mirrored by Lake Dove. Three thousand
millimetres of annual rainfall create an eerie
atmosphere felt by all who visit Cradle Mountain.
Gustav Weindorfer first stood on Cradle Mountain
in 1910 and was so overwhelmed by the beauty he
saw that he declared it must become a national
park — his dream was realized when it was
declared a national park in 1947 to preserve some
of Australia's most spectacular and diverse natural
heritage. Rugged plateaux, giant King Billy pines
and celery top pines loom above glacial tarns, dark
rainforests house rivers which thunder over sheer
cliffs and pour onto plains speckled by moss and
swamps and the rare pencil pine. Since December
1982 this region has been a World Heritage area in
recognition of its unique natural beauty, of habitats
where threatened plants and animals are able to
survive and for the valuable example it provides of
earth's evolutionary history.

A ghost gum stands silently over the abandoned buildings of the old telegraph station which once hummed with activity near Alice Springs. The settlement of Central Australia by Europeans began here, when the station was built as a vital link in the overland telegraph to transmit messages across the vast empty continent. The overland telegraph ran straight up the centre of Australia, from Adelaide to Port Darwin, and was completed in 1872.

The Hotel Albert in Monto, approximately 500km northwest of Brisbane, was built in 1830 by Arthur Albert Morgan as the last of a series of hotels this enterprising Australian built in inland Queensland. As the railway was built from Maryborough near the coast to the inland farming towns, Arthur Morgan built hotels along the track. The Hotel Albert is a typical Australian pub in every respect, except for one unusual feature. Arthur Morgan built a 'coffee room' as well as a dining room, which would seem unlikely to be popular with the wild men of the Queensland bush — but it was never empty. The pub has 32 bedrooms which were once booked out every weekend because the local farmers would come to have a drink on Friday night and not leave til Sunday.

The High Court of Australia in Canberra has been the centre of many famous legal battles and the site of some landmark judgments — it is Australia's highest court of appeal, the apex of the Australian judicial system. With the opening of the High Court Building in 1980, the Australian High Court was provided with a permanent home for the first time. The design of the building was the result of a national architectural competition held in 1972 and 1973. The building has three courtrooms, a public hall, Justices' rooms and an administration wing. The High Court looks over Lake Burley Griffin from its southeast shore and is made almost totally from reinforced concrete.

The Yulara Resort sits unobtrusively among the spinifex in the heart of Australia. Yulara is a small village in the desert, providing accommodation for every budget, from the luxury of the Sheraton Ayers Rock Hotel to the spacious Ayers Rock campground.

The resort was designed by Philip Cox, one of Australia's most inspired architects, and includes tennis courts, swimming pools, restaurants, bars and shops. Yulara is only 20km from Ayers Rock and 27km from the Olgas.

A sweeping view over Surfers Paradise, heart of the Gold Coast. Just an hour's drive south of Brisbane, Surfers is a full-on city with skyscraper beach flats crowding the golden sand and a hectic nightlife.

This peaceful scene is one of the few surviving visual reminders of Australia's convict past: Port Arthur, established in southern Tasmania as a prison town to provide the harshest punishment for the harshest prisoners. The ghostly white remains of the penitentiary were originally a flour mill and granary which were converted in 1853 to house 1000 prisoners from Norfolk Island. When built in 1844, the flour mill and granary were said to be the largest buildings in Australia.

The rock paintings of Arnhem Land are of central importance to Aboriginal culture. They are testaments to the close relationship the Aboriginal people have with the land and with their legendary past, the Dreamtime, when the ancestors created the world as they journeyed across Australia. The hard sandstone of the Arnhem Land escarpment makes perfect natural galleries for rock paintings. The rock paintings of Arnhem Land are among the most extensive and important examples of ancient art in the world. The best-known sites are at Obiri Rock and Nourlangie Rock, where spectacular examples of the famous 'X-ray' paintings can be found. These paintings are so named because they depict the internal parts of animals and humans. The rock paintings are painted with pigments made from clays, ochres and charcoals.

A golden trail of sun reaches across the floodplains of Ubiri in Kakadu National Park. The dramatic cycle of water shapes the appearance of Kakadu and creates two strikingly different seasons. The rains come during the summer Wet and are preceded by six months of Dry. In October or November the anticipation of rain reaches a climax and is finally rewarded when the skies burst forth and spill the rains across the parched earth and into the waterways. These waterways teem with life — nearly fifty species of fish are found in Kakadu, the barramundi being the most famous of these and over one-third of all Australia's bird species have been sighted by the waters of Kakadu. Over fifty species of native mammals come to drink from the rivers and billabongs and twenty-two species of frogs and 6,000 identified species of insects fill the skies with their evening songs. Kakadu is also home to a variety of plant life, which clusters around marshes and lily-padded waters, creeks and waterways to be close to permanent water. The outstanding richness of the plant and animal life of this region contributed to the declaration of Kakadu as a World Heritage site in 1981.

The unusual ochre and red sandstone tower of Chambers Pillar rises 34 metres into the clear desert sky, making it a prominent landmark from which early explorers were able to take their bearings. It lies 175km south of Alice Springs in a 340ha reserve declared in 1970. The pillar was named by John McDougall Stuart during his epic journey northward from Adelaide in 1860, after James Chambers who financed Stuart's expedition. The sandstone monolith is the result of millions of years of erosion, the remnant of an ancient plateau worn down by the harsh Australian environment. It was known as Itakaura by the desert Aborigines and holds an important place in Dreamtime legend.

This dramatic rocky coastal scene is typical of the coastline around Broome, in Western Australia. Rust red rock faces meet yellow sands under piercing blue skies and give way to the immensity of the Indian Ocean. These rocks mark the end of the Kimberley region, a land of fantastic contrasts, from sweeping cattle plains to rugged gorges and coastal cliffs, which are hit by wild tropical cyclones during the summer Wet.

The dramatic white sandstone towers of Carnarvon Gorge National Park loom out of a green and fertile jungle. Carnarvon Gorge is a small oasis breaking the dry flat monotony of central Queensland. Two million years ago the entire region of Carnarvon Gorge fell below the level of the surrounding plain and over millions of years the tilting, uplifting and erosion of the land created the truly awesome beauty of the magnificent landforms found in this national park. Carnarvon Creek runs through the Gorge, watering the plant and animal life that shelter below the gorge walls. The largest ferns on earth are found here, with fronds reaching up to 6m long — the King Fern is aptly named. Gums, bottlebrush, she-oaks, orchids and mosses flourish along the river and amongst them live wallabies, kangaroos, possums, wading birds, cockatoos and frogs.

The peaceful green of this South Australian scene attracted the early settlers to this third state of the young Australian colony after Charles Sturt had travelled down the Murray River to its mouth and had returned singing the praises of the fertile plains and picturesque ranges of this region.

South Solitary Island, a tiny desolate speck in the Pacific Ocean, off the north coast of New South Wales. During fierce storms, waves sweep over the 11ha of bare rock. On 5 March 1880, the 64m fortified concrete lighthouse shone its first beacon of light out over the Pacific Ocean. The light was possibly the first in New South Wales to use kerosene, which powered its 205,000 candelas until electricity was introduced. In 1975 the lighthouse keepers were withdrawn from this little rocky haven.

The eleven formations that make up the Glasshouse Mountains lie about 100km north of Brisbane. They are the solidified lava plugs of ancient volcanoes which have been eroded over time to expose their hardened cores. The highest mountain in the group is Mt Beerwah, named from the Aboriginal word meaning 'up in the sky', and is 556m tall. The rather exotic sounding name of the mountains actually has a more prosaic origin — the Glasshouse Mountains were so named by Captain Cook on his voyage along the East Coast of Australia in 1770 because they reminded him of the glass furnaces of Yorkshire, his home.

The dust storms that sweep through the desolate plains of South Australia are the legacy of man's attempt to grow wheat here — last century South Australia decided to become the wheat bowl of Australia, as it had no gold and was poorer in wool than the other states. Ignoring 'Goyder's Line' — a line drawn by the surveyor Goyder to indicate the geographical limits of viable wheat farming — the farmers pushed inland clearing the country and sowing wheat. After a few good seasons the rains eventually failed to come and the fallow land became dust which blew hither and thither leaving the land in ruins.

Coober Pedy lies to the north of the Nullarbor Plain in South Australia, an orange and brown desolate landscape, cratered and pockmarked and littered with rubble. European man inhabits this extraordinary outpost only because of the magnetic attraction held by the opals found beneath the barren earth, which have generated a multi-million dollar industry. With temperatures that can reach 54°C, most of the population of Coober Pedy lives underground, in cave-like dwellings that have led the aborigines to refer to the town as 'White Fella's hole in the ground'.

The lonely isolation of the Australian outback is contained in the name of this northern NSW town. 'Come-by-Chance' is a tin shed — the Memorial Hall — and a graveyard, 42km from Walgett. It was named by George and William Colless when in 1862 they bought a sheep station, by chance, in the district. Banjo Patterson wrote of this town: 'But my languid mood forsook me when I found a name that took me. Quite by chance I came across it — Come by Chance was what I read. No location was assigned it, nor a thing to help one find it. Just an N which stood for northward and the rest was all unsaid.'

LIFESTYLES

Australians live like no-one else in the world. Indulgent: a little. Hard: in patches. Outdoors: a lot. It is a land for living outdoors . . . on the beach, in the parks, in the bush. It is a society accused of being consumed by sport. Prime Minister Bob Hawke uses sport as his bridge to the middle-ground Australia voter.

For many years — before the Eastern Bloc used sport as a political tactic and took scientific sport to heart — Australia dominated world sport in a style out of all proportion to our numbers. Swimmers, tennis players, scullers, golfers, track and field . . . world champions or record holders would bob up regularly. Australian aggressiveness and competitiveness, together with a superb climate, created the opportunity for success. Sport, unlike art or politics, or even trade, gave the brash young country a chance to challenge on an equal footing. Equal, of course, until the advent of booster drugs and the transformation of sport into big business.

Sport is still fun in Australia. Aggressive fun but fun nevertheless. Cricketers too old, too chubby or perhaps just never good enough anyway play social cricket, some serious like Sydney's Greenwich Plate League which features former State players, actors, writers, cricket lovers; some pure Bacchanal where the cans of beer bowled over are much more important than the runs scored.

If Australia doesn't lead the world in sport itself, it is champion in sports television coverage. Naturally, cricket coverage is superb. Not everyone can make the team to play the West Indies but millions can watch the cameras (and the microphones) pick up every detail, however embarrassing. And a football grand final or the Melbourne Cup is a daylong event. One network starts its Melbourne Cup coverage virtually at dawn, and this for a 3min 20sec race run in the mid-afternoon. For hour upon hour experts and amateurs alike are given their chance to pick the winner; fashions are observed and picked apart like loose seams on a dress; old glories are relived; politicians parade for the cameras.

Perhaps the greatest indication of Australia's sporting drive is football. It is a divisive field with four codes vying for players. Australian Football dominates Western Australia, South Australia and Victoria. Rugby League is the sport which commands the main following in New South Wales and Queensland. Rugby Union has its followers also in New South Wales and Queensland. Soccer is an across-the-board sport with a major following in no State. Yet, in a country of only 16 million people, Australia has been world champions in both Union and League and done creditably on the world circuit in Soccer. Australian Football is just that, played here: nowhere else in the world. The game grew from a crude form of Gaelic Football played by miners on the Victorian goldfields in the 1850s. The Melbourne Football Club was formed in 1858, happily borrowing rules from other codes. In 1866 the first official rules were drawn up. Melbourne remains the focal point of the sport, even though a Sydney team, the Swans (formerly South Melbourne) was established in the 1980s to try to make inroads in the lucrative Sydney market. The code's following in Melbourne is phenomenal. Crowds of 80,000 regularly attend important matches; the MCG was crowded with 121,796 fans in 1970 for the grand final between rivals Carlton and Collingwood.

Perhaps, as Sydneysiders claim, the beach is too big a drawcard for football to ever dominate a Sydney weekend. But then the beach is a drawcard to virtually every Australian.

Tourists make Bondi an essential visit when they land in Sydney. It's a busy beach, not one of Australia's lazy, half-forgotten beaches flung carelessly on the coastline to dry in the summer sun. Bondi is for joggers, early morning exercisers, surfers, board riders and the locally famous Icebergs, a group of leathery old characters who swim every day. They're as much a fixture as the careless young beauties who always seem to lose the top half of their bikinis. Long after the sun sets on Bondi it shines magnificently in the west.

It's 5.30pm on a January afternoon at Cottesloe Beach, one of Perth's many beachside suburbs on the Indian Ocean. Australia is playing the West Indies in a day/night cricket match back in Sydney. And this day seems to sum up the Australian mix of sun, sand, sport and the pub. The lowering sun is casting an impossible silver shadow over the sea; it's slightly choppy and there's a good little breeze. Windsurfers are cutting and dancing across the chop. A container ship sits out at sea, waiting for a cue to come in, a four-masted sailing ship is going behind her. In the Cottesloe Beach Resort the boys from the beach are filtering in. The Australians have hit a staggering 100 runs off the first 16 overs; and this against the West Indian pace attack. It could be a great match. The boys take their seats, their cans and glasses and settle in to watch; singlets, T-shirts, board shorts, the odd pair of jeans. And somehow it seems to capture the ethos of an Australian summer.

It would be easy for visitors and casual observers to see Australia as just sport and the beach. But there is a remarkable mix of cultures and mini-cultures. The many and varied migrants have had substantial input: Melbourne is often said to be the third biggest Greek city in the world outside Greece itself; middle-Eastern migration has been substantial, Italians have transformed the face of food in delicatessens, supermarkets, restaurants and even the Aussie corner store now stocks pasta as a matter of course. Germans, Czechs, Dutch, Chinese, Indians, French, so many groups have had an effect on the changing face of Australia in the post-war period. And yet the remarkable fact is that the migrants have changed more than the country. Such is the strength of the Australian lifestyle based on climate and open spaces that the migrants have, in the main, found it more comfortable to adapt, rather than relive their own customs in some tiny pocket of a new land. So you find distinctively Italian names in the national cricket team, and the leading Australian Rules sides; Germans still have a strong hand in the Barossa Valley wine world of South Australia; middle Europeans from half a dozen countries live comfortably alongside one another in the opal fields; burly tattooed men with names as long as their trucks push giant road trains through the heartland of Australia, a transport lifeline to the Northern Territory and through the vast spaces of the West.

And in every corner of Australia, no matter where the people originally come from they all adopt the great Australian lifestyle tradition: the barbecue. In essence it is impractical and illogical — eating hot food outdoors with the flies for company on a 40°C day — and hardly gives the arteries and digestion an easy time. Food purists shudder at the sight of a barbie in full flight: sausages tortured on a hot plate, steaks considered well done when the charcoal disguises the meat, an oil-coated chicken looking as though it fell out of a bushfire. And all this washed down by neck oil: cans of Australian beer. Lots of cans of Australian beer! Healthy, no. Popular, yes. Across the country the barbecue is our social bridge. Cramped balconies on inner city flats can always squeeze in a portable barbie; boats on the harbour or the bay carry them, the barbie can always fold into the boot of a car or be thrown on the tray of the van. The ubiquitous barbecue. It's as close as we come to a national cuisine. Even the great Australian dish Vegemite is not really ours. Oh, we developed it, we made it infamous, but the US food giant Kraft now owns the product. Slowly Australia is developing a cuisine. The climate has played a dominant role: the European heritage of a White Christmas and roast turkey has been finally eclipsed. Roast dinners and heavy plum puddings wane on a day when even the flies are too exhausted by the heat to take much interest. The natural food wealth of the country and the climate are beginning to shape a distinctively Australian menu: seafood, particularly prawns and lobster, the myriad of tropical fruits, the clean crisp vegetables. All these are being shaped by superb chefs such as Gay Bilson of Berowra Waters, near Sydney, and Stephanie Alexander of Melbourne into a recognisable Australian pattern owing a little to France and lot more to adaptability and commonsense.

And if the face of food is changing the retail customs which helped forge patterns and lifestyles are not far behind. It was customary for many years to do the shopping on Thursday night (late night shopping) or Saturday morning. This fitted in with sport on Saturday afternoon and the beach on Sunday. But change is inevitable. In Sydney the major stores pioneered Sunday opening to meet the tourist demand it is said. The hours we work and shop are being changed by the relentless worldwide consumer demand.

Some people couldn't care less: the swagman still lives and plods happily ignorant of trading hours, union demands, tourism needs or whether the horseradish mayonnaise on the scampi had just a touch too much bite to it. Like World War I veterans their numbers are dwindling, but the swaggie can still be seen on the backroads. Men who don't give a fig whether the deregulated banking system has contributed to a rise in home interest rates, or whether the Australian dollar is a smidge too high against the yen. With healthy legs and an even healthier disregard for modern suburban and urban life they walk from town to town, casual job to casual job, old friends to new acquaintances. River banks provide a comfortable mattress and why have a pinched back yard with a wire cage around the pool when the old Outback is your yard and the rivers are not fenced-off.

Agricultural shows, royal or otherwise, still play a part in the Australian lifestyle. In the capital cities the show is a big deal: when urban youngsters often see farmyard animals for the first time. And sometimes the youngsters who have come in from the bush trade experiences: seeing the ocean for the first time. It's a

Taking a break from the bustle of the bar, the proprietors of an outback hotel in Winton, Central Queensland, relax on the verandah. The shire of Winton lies between Longreach and Cloncurry, and has a population of fewer than 2000 in its 53,820 sq km. The district was first settled in 1873 and the town was named by the first settler and postmaster, Robert Allen. Winton is the centre of a large merino sheep and beef cattle industry, with up to one and a half million sheep and over 61,000 head of cattle grazing on the surrounding pastures. Australia's national airline QANTAS was born in Winton and it was in Winton, in the North Gregory Hotel, that A.B. 'Banjo' Patterson's ballad Waltzing Matilda was first sung in public in 1895, having been composed on nearby Dagworth Station.

magical time for the city dwellers who go to see the magic of the country in action: to see dogs with an IQ higher than many lawyers round up sheep effortlessly, or stand in awe at the jams, pickled vegetables and cakes the country women make look easy. Log chopping and log sawing exhibitions and competitions, equestrian events, the judging of the magnificent stock animals brought in for the all-important blue ribbon. It's all part of the rich flavour. The country on parade has remained a constant delight; the sideshow alleys which invariably accompany the major agricultural shows have moved, sadly and tawdrily, with the times. Electronic machines compete with the traditional three-legged woman or the headless dog for hard-earned pocket money. The silicone chip mercilessly makes inroads on the noblest of traditions!

The world will go on changing but like the migrants who come here and adapt, the very nature of Australia will resist many of the developments. Mustering cattle and sheep on vast country stations has seen changes: motorcycles and helicopters have been introduced. But long cattle drives still rely on expert horsemen. In a way, it's similar to the traditional Sydney-Hobart yacht race. Technical refinements, computer innovations, the latest equipment: they've all been introduced but in the final analysis the ability of a group of men to stay alert and efficient for three, four, five days is the final test. Computers may predict the weather but they can't trim the boat, reef in a sail, handle the swell or counter sea sickness. A person is still the most efficient machine for handling the demands of Australia, on land or at sea.

In the High Country, that magnificent, little-visited zone of Australia — certainly underused in comparison with the Outback and the Reef — the technical revolution has made no impact. In the land that people came to know in modern times through the film *The Man From Snowy River* it might well be the turn of the century still. Horses are the means of transport from one log cabin to the next, the air is pure, the vegetation unspoilt. The High Country could become the last refuge for a life far from the crowds.

Other people have adapted to the influx of visitors to what were once badlands or at best, remote lands. The Outback was romantic and idealised but rarely visited; a zone that was loved best from a distance. Tourism, transport, technology have brought the Outback into modern travel budgets and schedules. A visit to the Camel King Noel Fullerton, for example, has become a popular event. Camels were introduced when Afghans came here to work on the Outback railway. They roam the Outback happily, at home in the sand and the heat.

But the High Country and the Outback are not where Australians actually live, certainly not in mass. The irony of life in Australia is that the romanticised image the world holds (and many Australians too) of the last frontier is lived by a handful of people. Fifty per cent of the population live in Sydney and Melbourne alone; less than 1 per cent of the country lives in that giant sprawling Northern Territory. Australia in fact is one of the most urban countries in the world; with more than 70 per cent living in the towns and cities clinging to the seaboard. A highly subjective quick whirl around the coastline highlights the love affair the bulk of Australians have for the water:

♡ Leaving the dubious delights of Bondi and past the genuine attractions of Pearl Beach, lies the Yuraygir National Park stretching for more than 50km along the coastline with 'secret' beaches hidden by headlands. It's a place for bushwalking, canoeing, surfing, fishing, relaxing. No crowds, no fighting for a square metre of sand to lay down a beach towel.

The face of Australia, of sun and sea and sand.

♡ Beyond the border, leaving behind Ballina, Tallows Beach and Byron Bay, lies the Gold Coast. Surfers Paradise is the focal point: too much lipstick and mascara but vivacious and eye-catching nevertheless. Surfers has another side to its golden beach with rolling waves and harbourside high-rise: the keys and canals created by man for leisure living. Here you see houses where the patio merges into the lawn running down to the edge of the canal. A seaplane sits at the pontoon just off the front lawn. Next to it is a cabin cruiser. The driveway at the side of the house holds a 4-wheel drive Landcruiser, a sporty compact, two kayaks, a jetski and the family sedan. This is keys living, Surfers style. A few minutes away lies Seaworld, an unabashed tourist show where dolphins jump through hoops before the water-skiers' ballet.

♡ Airlie Beach, gateway to the Whitsunday Passage, is an expensive, even over-rated strip of land. But beyond the booming township lies some of the most beautiful islands in the world. Tahiti's Bora Bora, described by James Michener as 'the most beautiful island in the world' won that title a little too easily. Certainly it is majestic, and certainly there are no imposing mountainous crags to match Bora's dominant peak, but the islands of the Whitsunday are remarkable. The same clear clean water as Tahiti, the same coral delights, and the sands are whiter and purer.

♡ Far North Queensland is the booming tourism playground. Film stars and sports stars (Lee Marvin and Jack Nicklaus) are regulars at the Cairns Marlin Meet, that September to December season when the giant black marlin cruise the waters outside the Reef.

♡ Further north, around Cape York and down into the Gulf of Carpentaria, a whole new world. No idyllic white beaches here: the white stretches spotted from the air as the plane circles Burketown are salt pans. This is barramundi territory — in the creeks not the salt pans!

♡ Around Arnhem Land and down into Darwin, the sparkling city built from the debris of Christmas Eve 1974 when Cyclone Tracy, which uprooted half the city's 11,000 homes and killed 66 people. The tropical climate has seen the gardens grow back stronger than ever; the resilient Territorians have rebuilt their city.

♡ West from Darwin, across the border into Western Australia and into Derby and Broome. The cattle shipping port for the properties of the Kimberley, Derby is also renowned for its boab tree with their grotesque trunks. Broome is further south, a mere 2250km from Perth. The pearling town which was once the booming centre of the north, Broome is being restored and developed.

♡ Rottnest Island, lying 19km off Perth, is a getaway favourite for the Western Australian capital residents. The island and its long beaches are sheltered by surrounding reefs which create excellent skindiving conditions.

♡   Leaving the Indian Ocean behind and racing across the Great Australian Bight, where the Nullarbor plunges abruptly into the Southern Ocean, into the Spencer Gulf and on to the Coorong, southeast of Adelaide. For nearly 200km this natural park throws up weird sand dune formations and provides a sanctuary for more than 150 bird species.

♡   Coorong is the route to the South Australian/Victoria border. Near the border is Portland, the first town settled in Victoria and now a fishing village where the local lobsters are sweet beyond belief.

♡   Closer to Geelong (and Melbourne) is the 300km of the Great Ocean Road, spectacularly clinging to the cliffs. This is the home of the lively Bells Beach, venue for major surfing competitions.

♡   Before leaving Melbourne for Gippsland, a fleeting visit to Tasmania. A coastline all its own, Tasmania is not the white sands and surf of many parts of mainland Australia. A line of small resorts on the east coast have beaches but in the main, Tasmania is craggy cliffs, sharply cut bays and pounding ocean swell. It has a majesty all its own.

♡   Back on the mainland, is the contrasting centre of Lakes Entrance, Victoria's most popular resort in summer but a sleepy little fishing village the bulk of the year. Gippsland has Australia's largest network of inland lakes stretching 70km behind the protection of Ninety Mile Beach.

That random sampling of the variety and depth of the coastline leaves so much unexplored. Australia is like that, too vast to reduce to a convenient series of descriptions.

The colours of the 'red centre' are reflected in the collection of sculptures made by William Ricketts for the Pitchi Ritchi Museum in Alice Springs. This series of unusual sculptures depicts the characters of the Aboriginal Dreamtime. Arranged in a large open space, amongst the gracious trees and red rocks of central Australia, these sculptures create a dramatic scene, evoking the mystery of the past they narrate.

Aboriginal culture has been affected in varying degrees by European settlement. Between the city dwellers and the tribes who live a traditional lifestyle are the nomads who set up 'white man camps' and brew up the billy.

The Aborigines of Cape York have a unique culture incorporating the myths of their ancestral heroes from the Torres Strait. A special ceremonial cockatoo-dance is performed in Cape York in remembrance of the ancestral hero Chivaree, and his brother, who travelled through the Torres Strait and came to Cape York. They first performed the ritual wearing magnificent head dresses of cockatoo feathers. Pearl shell pendants are made for this ceremonial dance and the men wear them on their painted chests.

The barbecue: Australia's al fresco eating style. And
here, in a Kimberly mining camp, there may not be
Rosemount Chardonnay and grilled quail but the
steaks and the snags taste great off the hotplate and
washed down with a tinny or three.

A swagman camped by a billabong — a quintessential part of the Australian bush. The swag is a sausage-shaped roll with a groundsheet or blanket on the outside wrapped around the swagman's worldly possessions. Swagmen were common during the nineteenth century and during the Depression, but today they are rare. Australian writer Henry Lawson spent some of his life travelling the outback as a swagman. One famous swagman, known as 'The Possum' because he slept in trees, died only a few years ago near Wentworth on the New South Wales and Victorian border. So respected was this old swagman that a statue has been erected in his memory in Wentworth.

Coober Pedy is the world's largest opal producing centre and one of the most inhospitable regions of Australia. The men and women who live here are hardy outback characters, although many of them are originally from Europe. Most of the population lives underground in former mining shafts — there is even an underground church. The name 'Coober Pedy' comes from an Aboriginal phrase meaning 'white fellers' hole in the ground'. The countryside around Coober Pedy is littered with the rubble dug up by fossickers, and is almost treeless.

Camel safaris are an increasingly common sight in central Australia — the perfect mode for exploring Australia's beautiful but dry and often inaccessible interior. Camels were first brought to Australia by Afghani camel men for expeditions into its desolate heart. Thirty-three camels from India were used by Burke and Wills on their expedition across Australia in 1860. Camels were later used to transport wool and other freight — each beast could carry a load of between 200 and 300kg — and to work on the transcontinental railway built in 1914.

The Camel King, Noel Fullerton, has 105 beasts at Alice Springs. Originally from Cooma, he moved to The Alice in 1967. From there he sets out on camel safaris lasting one to five weeks around Central Australia. 'Ninety eight per cent of my clients are women,' he says.

The colourful Alice Springs Lions' Camel Cup Carnival is held annually in May, making use of the thousands of wild camels that roam central Australia. The advent of railways and motor transport led to the demise of the camel as a means of transport, and most drivers let their animals loose in the desert. Today there are about 30,000 wild camels in central Australia.

The dusty plains of Bourke . . . home to a major cattle industry. Not much prospers out here on this flat dry expanse of land, except gigdee, a small Australian wattle which flourishes in the dry red dust. The cattle stations are immense, so the droving of stock from paddock to paddock is an important part of life in this region. This stockman wears the traditional bush uniform: an Akubra hat and a Driz-a-Bone, a waterproof oilskin. The ubiquitous Akubra is the classic Australian hat. Its name is derived from the Aboriginal word for head cover.

The famous outback centres of Australia are primarily cattle country — the Kimberley, the Gulf country, and the great stretches of the Northern Territory. The graziers bring their stock into the yards for special attention — for branding or to send them to market — otherwise leaving them to fatten on often vast open pastures. The Australian cattle industry is becoming increasingly sophisticated, with the introduction of video cattle auctions in 1984 and the first auctions of semen for breeding by artificial insemination.

The bullock train, once a major transport force in Australia, has been relegated to a curiousity.

The Royal Agricultural Show in Perth is held for a week round the end of September or beginning of October. Agricultural shows are major events for both city and country people in Australia — this is the time the outback comes to town. In each state capital the 'Show' is an annual event where the farmers and country people show their finest stock and agricultural produce, competing to win prizes and giving the city people a glimpse of outback life.

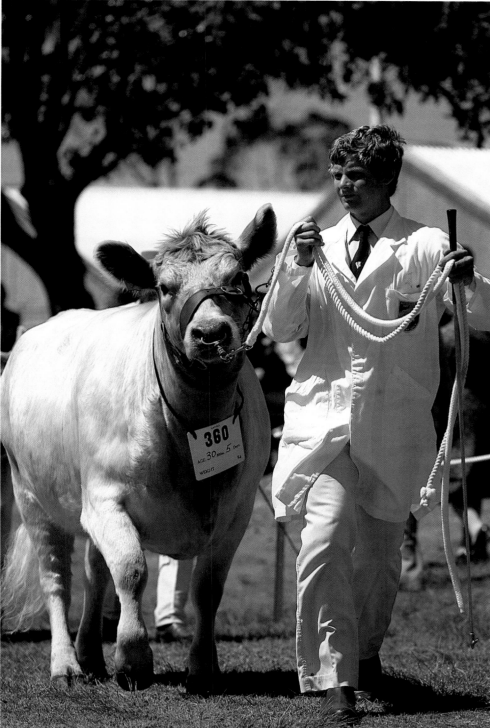

The western plains of Queensland support a flourishing sheep industry. The first sheep were brought to western Queensland from Goulburn by the Durack family last century. Today wool is still a major Australian export industry. These newly shorn sheep move slowly across the yard, free from their heavy woollen coats. Shearing is usually done after the winter months, when the wool has grown

thick to keep the animals warm. Until the late 1880s, sheep were shorn using hand shears, but a shearing machine was developed in Australia by Frederick York Woseley and the old click of the shears soon became a thing of the past as the whirring of the shearing machines took over. Australia's most famous shearer was from central Queensland — Jackie Howe who in one day sheared a record 321 sheep with hand blades.

Although the golden days of droving are over in Australia, the traditions and values of these rugged men and women live on in the Australian bush. Moving cattle in mobs over large distances is one of the most important features of the cattle industry, so it is not surprising that the drovers have become legendary. From the 1950s road transport and truck drivers began to replace the drovers, but even in 1987 at least eight mobs of 1800 head of cattle travelled from the Barkly Tableland down the western Queensland Georgina Stockroute to Glen Ormiston, a journey of about five weeks.

In the dry heart of Australia cattle are run on vast dusty plains. With an average rainfall of only 200mm the cattle stations of the Northern Territory must be enormous to survive, but they carry only a few cattle per square kilometre. These cattle belong to Hamilton Downs Station, which lies 75km north west of Alice Springs. It is 1807 sq km and carries 3,800 head of cattle.

The famous ballad 'The Man From Snowy River' was written by 'Banjo' Patterson in praise of the Australian mountain men and their horsemanship. In this soft mountain country the silence is disturbed only by the wind and the sound of horses' hooves — this is a land of horses, where brumbies roam the wild mountain peaks. These are easily the highest mountains in Australia, yet the highest peak, Mt Kosciusko, reaches an altitude of only 2,228m. In winter snow begins to fall around June and may cover as much as 7000 sq km in thick drifts.

A Barossa Valley farmhouse with the fondly
Australian iron roof atop white buildings standing
sentinel for rows of grapes. The Barossa, regarded
as a premier world wine-growing district, holds a
wine festival every two years, alternating with
Adelaide's biennial arts festival.

The cool crisp green of vine leaves in the Barossa Valley at Seppelts Winery, a hint of pleasures to come in the bottling season.

The afternoon sun filters through King Street, a
surprisingly quiet moment in the hectic Sydney
CBD.

The long lonely stretches of the Outback. Where a
truck can generate a dust storm of its own as it
pounds from one farflung town to the next.

The farmer, his dog . . . and a motorbike. The bike has moved in to challenge the horse in the large stations of the Outback. But the dog still has pride of place.

The soft-faced little kelpie — one of the grazier's most valuable possessions. It is one of the few breeds of Australian dog, a hardy sheepdog bred for its speed and intelligence. Developed from imported Scottish collies, the full ancestry of the kelpie is uncertain — it is thought to contain some dingo, which may explain its resilience in harsh Australian conditions. Kelpies are trained from an early age to help move sheep from paddock to paddock and to the yards for shearing, marking, mulesing and dipping.

It's a dog's life in Australia. . .but not for everyone.
The deck of a schooner at anchor in the harbour or
the bridge of a luxury cruiser sliding past the
Opera House are weekend indulgences.

The silver Indian Ocean off Perth Beach sparkles in
the evening light as optimistic fishermen try for a
lucky catch.

Brampton Island is a resort on the Great Barrier Reef, its crystal waters and calm seas make it a popular tourist destination. It is the southernmost of the Whitsunday islands, which were named by Captain Cook during his voyage up the east coast of Australia more than two hundred years ago. The island was first opened to tourists in the 1930s, who flocked to the cool of its lush tropical rainforests, the warmth of its white sandy beaches and the magnificent coral reef that fringes the island.

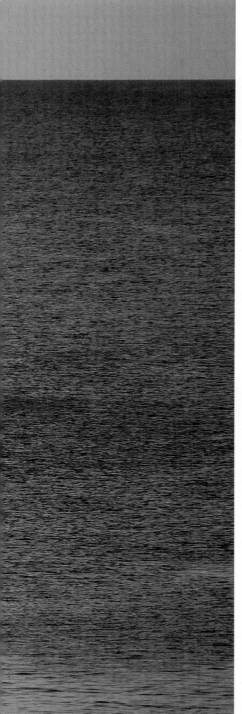

Land yachting, an Australian invention, takes the principles of skiff racing onto dry land. Given a smooth sandy surface the yachts skim along on their lightweight wheels. An Australian. championship was held during the Bicentennial celebrations at Lake Torrens in South Australia to raise money for the Royal Flying Doctor Service.

The famous surf and sandy stretch of Bondi Beach is only 8km from the hectic business centre of Sydney. Bondi is the home of the surf lifesavers, who formed their first association here in 1907 to patrol these sometimes hazardous waters, and of the Bondi Icebergs, a group of men who swim throughout the year, even in the icy winter waters. Bondi is named after its spectacular breakers, derived from an Aboriginal word meaning 'the sound of tumbling waters'.

The lifesavers of Australia's beaches are a national institution — the yellow and scarlet caps common throughout the summer months. Both girls and boys may join a life saving club from the age of seven, to train with the older members to become lifesavers.

In New South Wales, in October 1907, a group of Sydney men formed the Surf Bathers' Association. Concerned with the rising incidence of drownings in the surf due to the recently removed restrictions on daylight surfing, these men became the fathers of a now national institution of over 60,000 members, one of Australia's greatest traditions, the surf life saving clubs. Since 1907 there have been over 304,012 rescues made by volunteer lifesavers. There are now 248 surf life saving clubs, whose members patrol Australia's beaches on weekends and public holidays from October to Easter in their distinctive red and yellow caps. Traditionally, lifesavers were supported by a fleet of surf boats, but these days jet rescue boats and inflatable outboard motor-powered rescue boats have replaced the surf boats. Much of the rescue work carried out by these mobile units is co-ordinated by radio network and some stretches of the Australian coastline are patrolled by helicopter. In 1980 the first women were permitted to join surf clubs and in New South Wales alone there are now about 6,000 women lifesavers.

The VFL Grand Final of the Victorian League at the Melbourne Cricket Ground is the highlight of the Victorian sporting year. More than 100,000 people teem through the gates of the Ground to watch this climactic event. Australian Football is one of the few sports to have been invented in Australia — it was first played in 1858 by New South Wales cricket enthusiasts Thomas Wentworth Wills and Henry Colden Harrison to help keep cricketers fit during the winter months. The first serious match of Australian Football was held on August 7, 1858 in Melbourne between Scotch College and the Melbourne Church of England Grammar School. Two teams of 40 played on a huge field, but neither side scored after three games so the field size and team numbers were reduced. Today the game is based on teams of 18.

Australia's bloody convict past is recreated in this flogging at Old Sydney Town, a reconstruction of Sydney from 1788-1810. Soldiers and convicts, craftsmen and other first settlers relive early Australia in this authentically reproduced town. Offences committed in the colonies or on the journey out from England were punished by confinement in one of the penal settlements, hard labour, floggings or periods on the treadmill. Sentences of up to 300 lashes could be imposed on convicts. In one month in 1833 in NSW 2,000 convicts were convicted to 9,000 lashes.

The Silverton Hotel, 33km west of Broken Hill. During the 1880s Silverton was a booming silver mining town of 7000 people, and seven grand hotels lined its main street. This Hotel was built at that time, once serving as the town's post office. On the small bar inside the pub sits an enormous bone, with the following words inscribed on its side: 'Don't bite me, bite this'.

In the last week of September, the Royal Agricultural Show is held for ten days in Melbourne. One of the most popular events in any show is the woodchopping — a semi-professional sport at which Australians have excelled, often dominating world championships. The first recorded woodchopping events were held in Tasmania, around 1874. By 1891 tournaments carried large sums of prizemoney, and handicapping was introduced to balance the competitions. Famous Australian champions, such as Mannie McCarthy, Bill Johnston, Tom Kirk and Jack O'Toole, were able to beat men half their age — woodchopping is a strenuous sport, but it also requires the great skill that comes with age and experience.

The tranquil turquoise of a reef island makes the Great Barrier Reef one of Australia's most precious jewels. Green Island is a tiny coral cay only 24km northeast of Cairns, one of the few true coral islands to accommodate tourists. Its sparkling white coral and lush green vegetation is easily accessible by boat from Cairns. Green Island has a magnificent underwater observatory and a marine museum, making it the most popular place from which to view the coral of the Barrier Reef.

The distinctive skyline of Sydney can be seen etched on the horizon from Watson's Bay, one of Sydney's loveliest harbourside suburbs on the southern headland. Sydney Harbour is the playground for all varieties of water craft, from windsurfers and catamarans, to the grandest of yachts and floating restaurants.

The Gold Coast of Queensland — one of Australia's fastest growing tourist areas, 32km of sea, sand and sun stretching from Coolangatta to Surfers Paradise. Sea World at Surfers Paradise is one of the many distractions that have sprung up to entertain the holidaymakers who flock here throughout the year. Sea World offers water spectacles of all varieties, from performing dolphins to lavish waterskiing displays.

FAUNA AND FLORA

Australia's face to the world is the extraordinary fauna and flora: those endearing koalas so often wrongly labelled koala bears, the kangaroo Australians take for granted but the rest of the world regards with fascination. The frilled lizard and the flying fox. The exotic birds and erotic flowers. The surly dingo and the sweet boronia. Ghost gums and Tasmanian devils.

But perhaps the most intriguing is the platypus which has taken a back seat in recent times. Other species have captured public interest. Perhaps because the platypus is by nature a shy and retiring animal; perhaps because it is nocturnal . . . whatever the reasons the platypus is becoming the forgotten curiosity of Australia. And yet this egg-laying mammal is an Australian treasure.

Only three monotremes — the earliest mammals — survive in the world. Two are species of echidna (one found only in Papua New Guinea), the other the platypus. Monotreme fossils have been found only in the Australian portion of Gondwana, the one-time super-continent. Although the echidna and the platypus are related the platypus followed a diverse evolutionary line, taking to the water. It developed a streamlined body coated with dense brown fur. The platypus uses its front paws, with their webs, as paddles to swim and the hindfeet act as rudders. The most remarkable feature of the platypus is its snout: a radar if you like, which detects its prey by sensing tiny electromagnetic fields surrounding the victim. The platypus moves along the bottom of rock pools and streams, its beak in the silt 'sounding' for worms and crabs. A mammal which lay eggs, the female encases her two eggs between her belly and her broad tail, breathing warm humid air on them to help them incubate. She holds this unconventional — and presumably uncomfortable — position for about ten days after the eggs are laid.

Less retiring is the kangaroo. Along with the koala the kangaroo is a worldwide Australian symbol. The coiled mainsprings they call hindlegs catapulted the kangaroo across the vast inland plains and into international recognition. That endearing leap was born as a simple defence mechanism; with one giant spring they could evade predators who discovered their hiding places.

The koala, an herbivorous marsupial, is the character of the Australia bush. Koalas live on the leaves of certain types of eucalypts and their lives have revolved around these eucalypts and their numbers threatened as urbanisation sees their simultaneous habitat and food source numbers reduced. Like the platypus, they are nocturnal. At daybreak they curl up in the fork of a tree, their round plump bottoms firmly planted in a comfortable crook and their fluffy backs resting on a limb. It is then they look at their most lethargic. Even decadent as they seem to sneer at the rest of the world hurrying by.

There is so much more to Australia fauna than these three species. The koala is one of more than 100 species of marsupial, in turn part of the 230 mammals found in the island continent. There are about 520 species of reptiles and amphibians (140 snakes, 360 lizard species making up the vast majority) and more than 50,000 insect species. The birdlife is varied and rich, more so than most countries with more than 700 species. They in turn thrive in harmony with the 12,000-plus species of flowering plant.

Overseas visitors and often, Australians themselves, have an image of the country as having dangerous, even lethal, species behind every gum tree and every rock. Certainly there are deadly creatures in this vast land — and in its waters. But their 'strike ratio' is almost non-existent. And some creatures which look deadly are in fact harmless. The poor thorny devil is far from lethal. A shy dragon-lizard the thorny devil is covered in spikes, giving it a fearsome appearance. But the only one to fear it should be the ant — thorny lizards are capable of eating 5000 at a single 'sitting'. The dingo, despite the much-highlighted Azaria Chamberlain case, has had very few reports levelled at it of attacks on humans. And the funnel-web spider, the subject of tabloid hysteria every summer, is in reality unlikely to bite unless trapped.

The Tasmanian Devil and the Tasmanian Tiger may have contributed to the image of ferocious Australia. Their names, after all, hardly conjure up pictures of newborn lambs dancing on green velvet pastures. But the Tasmanian Tiger is almost certainly extinct although some naturalists believe in rare reported sightings. The Tasmanian Devil, despite his name, its appearance and its howling is friendly. A loner, the Tasmanian Devil hunts by night, crushing its prey in its large jaws.

The dingo (*Canis familiaris dingo*) is Australia's most powerful predator and is found in the scrub and semi-desert environments of the continent. It is believed that the Aborigines brought the dingo to Australia from Asia around 5000 years ago. The dingo is a very early form of dog — its paws are larger than a normal dog's and its triangular ears remain erect. It cannot bark like a dog and it breeds only once a year, with both parents caring for the young. The longest fence in the world, the 9660km Dog Fence, was built across eastern Australia to prevent the dingo from preying on sheep.

Newly discovered in Australia is the fierce snake, thought to be the deadliest snake in the world. Very little has been discovered about the snake although it is thought to be a close relative of the taipan and its venom is the most toxic yet analysed. Fortunately it seems to be in small numbers and restricted to the inland eastern Australian region, a sparsely populated area. The fierce snake is one of about 124 snake species; among the reptiles lizards are much more widespread and varied. They range from tiny skins to the perentie at more than 2m in length. The most popular of the lizards is the frilled lizard. With ruffs of frill around his neck he is a smallish, relatively innocent looking creature until threatened. Then he opens his mouth which has the effect of fluffing up the frill to make him appear substantially larger to a would-be predator. To be on the safe side he sways from side to side, hissing. But his appearance is only part of his unusual nature; if he turns to flee or is, in turn, a predator chasing some insect he races on his hind legs like an awkward bird but generating a fair turn of pace.

Australia's wildlife lives in a diversity of habitats: deserts, the oceans, rivers, plains, forests — and mangrove swamps.

❀ The unprepossessing mangroves are a lifestyle all their own. Dank dark mud clings to the multi-rooted mangroves, sandflies and mosquitos are thick in the steamy sky, ghost crabs dance furtively across the knobbled ground and down to the water's edge as the sun sets. Soldier crabs, semaphore crabs, blue swimmer crabs and the fiddler crab with its lone orange claw . . . the mangroves are their home.

❀ The coastal section of the Alligators River region just outside the Kakadu National Park is virgin wetland, rich in birdlife. Many tropical waterbirds such as the pied goose, the wandering whistling duck and the pygmy goose have found refuge here. Large flocks of pelicans join the ducks in a cacophony of sound. Doves, pigeons, wrens, honeyeaters and lorikeets thrive here. A howling jackass — a member of the kookaburra family — perhaps a black falcon or a magnificent sea eagle . . . all part of the life here, are additional delights.

❀ The abundance of the wetlands is abruptly different in the 'drylands' . . . the fringes of the Simpson Desert. Feral camels, dingoes, donkeys and brumbies thrive in the near-barren surroundings. Black-faced wood swallows share this wilderness with them; surviving for long periods without water.

❀ But in the far south . . . in Tasmania's south-west wilderness, water shortages are far from a problem. And the heat of the Simpson is another world away: instead, an icy wind cuts in from the Antarctic and a drizzly rain keeps it company. Unlike the Simpson this is a rain-soaked land with more than 3000mm falling a year. Oystercatchers, kelp and jellyfish thrive on the coastline cut and battered by the southern seas.

❀ The high country of Victoria is another rainfall zone (2400mm a year). But here the rare mountain pygmy possum deer and foxes rule, scampering among the alpine herbs and shrubs. Yellow paper daisies and minute alpine daisies bring mini-splashes of colour to the slopes of the inhospitable ridges.

The flora of Australia: it's remarkable. But not because it so colourful or exotic, although it can be. More because it so adaptable. Australia's unforgiving climate puts hard demands on nature's capacity to survive. The eucalypts are Australia's most characteristic plant, more than 500 species survive in habitats as diverse as bleak mountain ridges and desert sands. The key to their success is their ability to survive fire: the perennial threat to Australian fauna and flora. Eucalypts found the answer in fanning the flames! Eucalypt leaves are rich with flammable oils. When fire sweeps through a region it burns fiercely, fed by the oils, but quickly, passing through a eucalypt zone rapidly, burning the leaves and charring the tree but leaving it to survive. The sapwood is protected by thick bark and lying safe under the bark is a reserve of leaf buds which shoot quickly following a blaze. The eucalypt lives on. In the desert, too, nature has learnt a survival mechanism. Water is scarce and the plants that spring up following rain have evolved to produce vast quantities of seed — enough to survive and to lie dormant until the next rains. Some desert species virtually shut down during prolonged periods of drought. Their metabolic processes go on slow, almost on hold, until the next lifegiving shower. The most striking of the desert blooms is Sturts's desert pea, the emblem of South Australia. Rain will transform the desert into a carpet of vivid red bells with shiny black tongues.

The flora of Australia flourished and evolved in the period following the split of Gondwana. Eighty per cent of Australia's plant species are endemic — they appear nowhere else in the world naturally. The floral face of Australia is marked by eucalypts in dense or open forest and in scrubland. Acacias which are almost as widespread as eucalypts pop up as wattles in woodland or as mulga in arid belts. Together these two generic groups form the character of Australia. The openness of the Australian bush is a distinguishing feature of the landscape. Gum trees shed little shade because of the shape of their leaves and the way they point down to the ground. Most of Australia's flora is adapted to arid or semi-arid conditions.

Rainforests form small pockets of the island continent's flora colony. Sadly, they are diminishing further as man makes inroads in the name of progress. The Great Divide generates enough rain to nurture these pockets on the eastern coast. They range from the majestic stands of southern beech in the far south of Tasmania fed by seemingly continuous mists and cold rain to the luxuriant tropical rainforests of far north Queensland where a combination of red basalt soil and annual rainfall of 4000mm creates the steam bath conditions they need to flourish. But perhaps the temperate rainforest with its generally cool climate and abundant rainfall presents the most interesting face of the varied rainforests in the continent. There is a seemingly greater diversity of tree species than in the far south or north. Coachwood, crabapple, dwarf cypress, lemon-scented tea-tree, blue gum, white hazelwood, walking stick palms, cabbage palms and elkhorn ferns all vie for their place in the jigsaw. Climbing plants twine around the trees, struggling to reach the canopy and the sun. Logs covered with moss litter the

The huon pine (*Dacrydium franklinii*) is found in the temperate rainforests of Tasmania along its rivers, lakes and swamps — its small leaves press close to its stems and tiny cones. The Huon Pine can often reach over 100 metres tall, especially in the south west of Tasmania where the temperatures are mild and the rainfall abundant.

forest floor. Unlike the general open face of the Australian bush little light filters through to the forest floor. Seedlings wait expectantly for a hole in the growth to emerge — for a forest giant to crash perhaps — and give them their chance to reach for the sun. There is an unreal stillness in this temperate rainforest: a cool light, a hush, a timelessness among the shadows.

How different to walk through Kakadu National Park, where openness is a way of life. A ghost gum grows almost impossibly from a crack in the escarpment. Paperback trees, savannah grasslands, heathlands, mangroves, sedgelands that can survive six months' submersion in the wet season . . . Kakadu and Arnhem Land have a variety of faces. Along the floodplains a network of billabongs give life to a variety of fauna and flora. This can be a land of colour and exotica: of giant lilies and lotus lilies, cockatoo apples, hibiscus and flame tree, fringe myrtle and water snowflakes. Ironically, one of the most striking species is love in the mist passionfruit, a South American import. Much of the Northern Territory flora has come in from further north, either wind or bird-borne.

This ancient zamia palm (*Macrozamia moorei*), whose origins can be traced back over 50 million years ago to the great supercontinent Gondwana, is found in central Queensland and northern New South Wales. It is a large palm like plant which grows to 5m with a thick trunk and leaves which may reach a metre long. The zamia palm produces orange seeds and a toxic nut as well as a fruit poisonous enough to kill most animals, except the emu which is specially adapted to feed on these fruits.

The rocky outcrops of Central and Western
Australia are home to this shy marsupial, the black-
footed rock wallaby (*Petrogale lateralis*). The rock
wallabies are a special group of wallabies perfectly
adapted to their rocky habitats. The soles of their
feet are studded to enable them to grip onto the
rocks, and their long tails help them balance as
they leap about their rocky homes. This is one of
the most beautiful of Australia's macropods — its
striking black and white markings help to
camouflage it in the shadows and shades of its
rocky playground from its most powerful predator,
the wedgetailed eagle.

The rare nocturnal platypus (*Ornithorhynchus anatinus*) is found in the freshwater lakes and streams of eastern Australia. The platypus is one of two monotremes in Australia — the echidna is its fellow survivor — and unlike other mammals it lays eggs, a characteristic inherited from its reptilian ancestors. When evening falls it leaves its burrow to hunt for worms, frogs and crayfish, which it stores in its cheek pouches to eat on the surface of the water — it consumes over two-thirds of its body weight in this manner. The platypus is adapted perfectly to its watery environment — its streamlined body is covered with thick brown fur for insulation and to enable it to swim quickly through the water; its front paws are webbed and used to paddle while the back feet are partially webbed and used for steering. Its snout is its most important sense organ, for beneath the water its eyes, ears and nostrils are closed. A special sensory device in its bill detects the electromagnetic field of its prey and is the platypus' sole guide to its food. The adult male has a poisonous spur on his hind feet which he uses in battles with other males

The red kangaroo (*Macropus rufus*) is Australia's largest macropod — a plain-dwelling creature that stands taller than a man when it rears up and balances on its powerful tail, this marsupial grows from 2cm at birth to over 2m tall. Although it is known as the 'red' kangaroo, most of the does and some of the bucks are actually blue-grey and are known as 'blue fliers'. Red kangaroos feed at night to avoid the hot sun and spend their days under shady trees and shrubs, lying in small depressions they dig for themselves. When travelling long distances — the red kangaroo moves in elegant bounds moving swiftly across the plains using its tail as a counterbalance it can reach speeds of up to 65km/h.

Young Tasmanian Devils (*Sarcophilus harrisii*) leave their mother's pouch at about 15 weeks and stay in their nest for another 15 weeks before accompanying their mother to forage for carrion. The devil is a scavenger, a solitary nocturnal animal named because of its hellish howling and devilish appearance. Once found throughout Australia, Australia's largest carnivore marsupial is now found only in Tasmania. Its extremely powerful jaws enable it to crush the bones of the large animals it feeds on, but despite its name and its jaws, the devil is quite a friendly and approachable creature. During the day the Tasmanian Devil can be found asleep in cool dark caves, rock crevices or hollow logs.

The spotted-tailed quoll (*Dasyurus maculatus*) is one of the largest of the surviving marsupial hunters, prowling the forests of eastern Australia. It is also known as the tiger cat — a fitting name for this ferocious predator, which kills its prey by biting it on the back of the neck or head with its strong sharp teeth and claws. These nocturnal animals are solitary creatures, only socializing at breeding time when it may mate for up to eight hours. The quoll has no permanent pouch — it develops folds of skin around the mammary area during the breeding season to feed its young.

The nonchalant koala (*Phascolarctos cinereus*) is Australia's most popular bush character. This mainly nocturnal creature inhabits the dry eucalypt forests and woodlands of eastern Australia. The only aboreal marsupial with no visible tail, it uses its strong claws to climb about the eucalypt trees which it makes its home. The koala feeds on only about seventeen species of the nearly 600 documented species of eucalypts, and has developed an elaborate digestive system which enables it to detoxify and eat the eucalyptus leaves poisonous to most other animals. Leaves supply the koala with everything it needs for sustenance, including water (it doesn't drink) except minerals, so for a mineral supplement to its diet of leaves the koala also eats small quantities of soil.

The superb lyrebird (*Menura Novae-hollandiae*) is one of Australia's most talented mimics — the mating of the lyrebird has an elaborate ritual of songs and dances held on one of the display mounds the males build in their territories. The males visit their display mounds during the breeding season from May to August. The ritual begins with seductive soft singing and a display of the bird's magnificent lyre-shaped tailfeathers, which swathe its body in silver plumage. The bird then dances and sings, singing its own song and the songs of other birds in the bush. Densely forested, dimly lit gullies are the favourite haunts of these large songbirds, which can grow up to a metre tall.

Commonly known as the Major Mitchell cockatoo,
this lovely pink cockatoo (*Cacatua leadbeateri*)
lives in the wooded banks that line the desert rivers
of arid and semi-arid Australia. The pink cockatoo
selects one partner for life, and the bond they forge
is strengthened by mutual preening and elaborate
courtship rituals. Both parents feed and care for the
young. The female cares for the eggs by night and
the male watches them during the day. The
spectacular crest of the pink cockatoo is raised
when the bird is excited — it is scarlet in the
centre with a thin yellow band and white tips.

The raucous laughing of the laughing kookaburra (*Dacelo novaeguineae*) is the theme song of the Australian bush. The kookaburra is the largest kingfisher in the world, growing up to 46cm long — its size enables it to hunt rats, lizards and small snakes as well as insects and mice, it will even dive into shallow water for prey. This sociable bird lives in a communal breeding society, a phenomenon more common among Australian birds than among any others, where the parents and other relatives of several generations stay together to help incubate the eggs and care for the young. The laughing call of the kookaburra is heard at dawn and sunset as the birds advertise the bounds of their extended family's territories.

The emu (*Dromaius novaehollandiae*) is Australia's largest bird and can be found wandering over most of Australia, its body swaying over the sun-bleached plains. The long legs and light body of the emu particularly adapt it to its nomadic life and its double-layered feathered coat helps to protect it from the fierce sun. This curious bird eats mainly leaves, flowers, fruits, seeds and insects, but it also eats pebbles and charcoal to help it grind its food. The male is responsible for incubating the eggs, rarely leaving the nest for the eight-week incubation period, and for bringing up the young — the female rarely stays to see her 8 to 10 large green eggs hatch, preferring to go off to mate with another male.

In arid inland Australia lives an unusual creature —
the rare burrowing frog (*Neobatrachus sp.*) which
has developed a sophisticated mechanism for
survival in the dry land. These desert frogs are
survivors from the time when central Australia was
a lush oasis and probably have adapted to the
desert by avoiding it. The burrowing frog buries
itself below the dry desert surface for up to five
years at a time in a cocoon-like skin to protect its
soft skin and to help prevent water loss. Two small
tubes run from the frog's nostrils through its
cocoon to allow it to breathe during its long sleep.
When the rains finally arrive they soak into the
burrow and awaken the frog which immediately
leaps to activity, climbing from its cocoon to join
the other frogs to breed in the rain. Within a month
there is a new frog generation ready to burrow
down again below the desert floor.

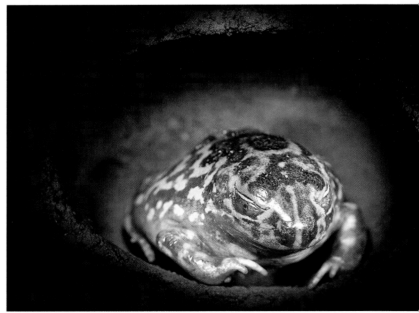

The freshwater crocodile (*Crocodylus johnstoni*) inhabits the waterholes and fresh water rivers of northern Australia — this preference for fresh water and its narrow smooth snout distinguish the Johnstone's crocodile from its more ferocious relative, the saltwater crocodile. These crocodiles reach only 2m or so long, compared to the 6m of the saltwater crocodiles, and feed on birds, frogs, fish, shellfish and other small animals. During the dry season the females nest, laying about 12 or so eggs on a river bank which hatch with the Big Wet and the abundance of food this season brings. The Johnstone's crocodile has a bony formation in its scales which distinguishes it from all other crocodiles in the world.

This very rare frog is endemic to SouthEast Queensland, confined to the wet gum forests and rainforest streams of the Conondale Ranges near Brisbane. The gastric brooding frog (*Rheobatrachus spp*) has developed a most unusual reproductive technique — it broods its eggs in its stomach, miraculously preventing its digestive juices from damaging the eggs. When the eggs have hatched, the tadpoles develop in the mother's stomach and the young frogs leave their mother's body through her mouth. The frog has not been seen since 1981, and is possibly extinct.

The Frilled Lizard (*Chlamydosaurus kingii*) is one of Australia's most spectacular reptiles, living in the dry forests and woodlands across northern Australia. The distinctive frill of the lizard opens out when it is alarmed, as a bluff to increase its apparent size and possibly as a form of heat regulation. The frill normally sits in folds around the lizard's neck, but unfurls when the lizard opens its mouth. When threatened, the lizard darkens in colour, stands on its back legs and rocks from side to side slowly hissing — a formidable sight. The forest floor provides insects and other small animals for the lizard to eat, which it chases with its distinctive and rather strange gait: using only its hind legs, the lizard scuttles across the ground looking like a peculiar bird.

The Fierce snake (*Paradamansia microlepidota*) has only recently been discovered and is found in the hostile sparsely inhabited savannah grasslands of inland eastern Australia. It is possibly the world's most venomous snake — its venom is the most toxic ever analysed. The rare Fierce Snake is not yet well-documented, but it is thought to be closely related to the taipan. Growing up to 2.5m long, this swift moving snake hides in cracks in the soil from where it hunts its prey.

The lace monitor (Varanus varius) is the largest predator in the Australian bush, and the second largest Australian lizard (the Perentie is the largest). Lace monitors can grow to more than 2m — this one is 1.5m long. They are powerful hunters, roaming the wet and dry forests and woodlands of eastern Australia, but spend most of their time motionless, camoflagued amongst the foliage of the bush. Lace monitors are good climbers and do much of their hunting in trees, where their long forked tongues probe tree hollows for sheltering mammals and birds.

The thorny devil (*Moloch borridus*) is actually a shy and harmless dragon-lizard — growing to about 15cm long, it lives quietly amongst the spinifex and sand of Central Australia eating ants. It is named for the thorny spikes which cover its body, giving it a ferocious facade to deter its predators. This day-time creature is perfectly adapted to its desert environment, which provides it with the challenges of harsh temperatures and low rainfalls. To combat the heat and cold of the desert climate, the thorny devil can change colour as the temperature varies — in the cool of the morning the lizard is a dark brown to absorb the heat, while in the middle of the day it pales to a lighter shade to reflect the heat. The scarcity of water has led the devil to make use of every molecule of available moisture for nourishment, even dew drops, which it does by channelling the drops to its mouth through a network of furrows carved into its skin. This little lizard has an enormous appetite — it can eat 5,000 ants at one sitting, eating about two ants a second.

The Murray Cod (Maccullochella peeli) is found in the freshwater rivers of all Australian states except Tasmania — it was introduced to Western Australia from the eastern states. Largest of the Australian native freshwater fishes, the Murray Cod has weighed in at 113.5kg and can grow to 1.8m. The fish is named after the Murray-Darling River system where it was once abundant in the sluggish waters. The damming and regulation of the Murray has made it difficult for the migratory Cod to survive, as the routes to its traditional breeding waters have been blocked off.

The rare and endangered Queensland Lungfish (Neoceratodus forsteri) is found only in Queensland, in the fresh waters of the Burnett and Mary Rivers. When first classified scientifically the lungfish was considered an amphibian because its massive tail is an apparent continuation of its body and its paired fins resemble limbs — it belongs to another age. It has a skeleton of cartilage rather than of bone, unlike modern fish. The lazy lungfish breathes through gills, but if the oxygen level of the often stagnant water where it lives drops too low it must rise to the surface to gulp air. Able to survive out of water for several days if kept moist, the lungfish spends most of its time searching for the crustaceans, worms and molluscs it eats.

This endangered ghost bat (*Macroderma gigas*) makes a ghostly silhouette in the tropical forests it haunts. Known also as the False Vampire, it is a large carnivorous bat and eats small mammals, lizards, frogs and birds. The ghost bat hunts at night, dropping out of the sky and enfolding its prey in its membraneous wings before killing it by biting the head and neck and then devouring it. The female bears a single offspring in the spring.

This extraordinary and rare marsupial mole (*Notoryctes typhlops*) is perfectly adapted to its desert environment — able to 'swim' through the desert sands searching for insects and small reptiles, like a tiny bulldozer this blind creature burrows through the earth. It has no ears, just small holes, and its nose is protected by a horny layer of skin which enables it to dig efficiently to about 2m or more.

This deadly poisonous funnel web spider (*Atrax versutus*) is found in the Blue Mountains and ranges of central New South Wales and is commonly known as the Blue Mountains funnel web. It is a heavily-built, tree-dwelling spider, living in tree hollows or under logs in a silken tube-funnel with silk curtains hanging over the entrance. The funnel web may set sticky silk trap wires on tree trunks to snare beetles and tree frogs. During the winter months when food is scarce the spider hibernates, coming to life again in the warm summer sunshine. The Blue Mountains funnel web is less aggressive than the Sydney funnel web, but equally as venomous, and will bite viciously only if trapped.

The highly venomous red-back spider (*Latrodectus mactans hasselti*) is found in many parts of Australia, in sheltered nooks and crannies around domestic buildings and gardens. The young spiders are a creamy colour with black-spotted abdomens while the adults have thin legs and globular abdomens with red or orange markings above and below. The female spider injects a poisonous venom into its prey which kills large insects, other spiders, small lizards and sometimes even young mice, bats and birds as well as being dangerous to humans. The red-back is a nocturnal hunter, sheltering by day in a tubular web that leads off a trap built to entangle the spider's prey. The adult spiders usually die after summer and by autumn hundreds of baby spiders hatch, floating off on parachutes of their own silk to start their first webs.

The karri (*Eucalyptus diversicolor*) is one of the largest trees in the world and may grow up to 90m. Famous for its timber, the distinctive smooth greyish bark and tall straight boughs of this tree grace the slopes of southern Western Australia.

Along the coastal swamps of Western Australia this
beautiful swamp paperbark (*Melaleuca
preissiana*) is found growing by the water. The
swamp paperbark has narrow elliptical leaves and
bursts into a mass of white spikey flowers in
summer and early autumn.

This beautiful inland tree is the signature eucalypt
of central Australia and yet it is also found in
neighbouring New Guinea — a legacy of the great
continent Gondwana. The ghost gum (*Eucalyptus
papuana*) grows up to 16 metres, its pendulous
leaves and branches gracing the harsh blue skies of
the red centre. The smooth white bark of this aptly
named tree has inspired many painters of the
Australian deserts, including Sidney Nolan, Arthur
Boyd and Fred Williams.

In the dry woodland scrub of Northern Queensland the beautiful deep pinky red of the Cooktown Orchid (*Dendrobium bigibbum*), Queensland's floral emblem, is found flowering in winter. This Australian orchid produces showy curving flower stems lined with deep cerise butterfly-like flowers with a texture of crepe paper.

PREVIOUS PAGE:
This tree is perhaps the most striking feature of the Australian bush in summertime. Known as the grass tree (*Xanthorrhoea australis*), it is slow to grow and may take five years before a recognizable clump of grassy foliage has sprouted, and up to 10 years before a flower spike shoots up. The flower spikes may grow up to five metres tall and look like black-tipped native spears until they burst into masses of tiny strong scented cream flowers.

Sturt's Desert Rose (*Gossypium sturtianum*), or
the red centred hibiscus as it is also known, is the
floral emblem of the Northern Territory and grows
on rocky slopes and gorges and in stony or sandy
soils along drainage lines in arid Australia. This
shrub may grow to 2m tall, producing hibiscus-like
flowers of a pale bluish-purple with red centres.

The common heath, (*Epacris impressa*) sometimes
known as the native fuchsia, is the floral emblem of
Victoria. It is a straggly shrub that grows to one
metre and flowers throughout the year — its
tubular flowers range in colour from white to pinks
to deep red.

Waratah, meaning "seen from afar", is the Aboriginal name for this striking red flower which is the floral emblem of New South Wales and is protected under the National Parks and Wildlife Act. Known as the New South Wales waratah (*Telopea speciosissima*), this shrub grows on the sandstone hillsides of the coast or highlands of New South Wales. The flower grows to 15cm in spring and can be seen at a great distance, hence its name.

Sturt's Desert Pea (*Clianthus formosus*) flourishes its dazzling red flowers only after heavy desert rains have spilled across the dry earth. It sends green tentacles out over the sands and shoots out its brilliant red bells with glistening black tongues. The floral emblem of Southern Australia, the desert pea is native to the dry outback regions of the continent.

The beautiful green kangaroo paw (*Anigozanthos manglesii*) is the floral emblem of Western Australia and grows in the sandy soils of the heaths and coastal plains of western and southern Western Australia. The brilliant forest green flowers are split almost to their base, revealing an exotically coloured centre and red stemmed flower spikes, which can reach one metre long.

The lovely waxflower is found in the cool eastern forests and alps of south-eastern Australia and is commonly known as native daphne. The long-leaf waxflower (*Eriostemon myoporoides*) is the most popular of the waxflowers — its beautiful star-like flowers, which are pink in bud and become white, blossom in spring and fill the air with a sharp citrus perfume. The flowers grow on a rounded bush with smooth narrow leaves.

The sticky boronia (*Boronia anemonifolia*) is a dainty shrub found in Queensland, New South Wales and Victoria. It flourishes in heaths and dry forests, where vegetation is thick and some shade is provided. It has slender leaves with three leaflets and tiny four-petalled flowers — its aromatic foliage makes it one of Australia's most desirable plants.

The broad-leaf tea-tree (*Leptospermum grandifolium*) is an endemic Tasmanian species, found in Tasmania and Victoria, with slender seeds and large pretty flowers. The common name 'tea-tree' is derived from the practice of the early settlers of soaking the leaves of this tree in boiling water to make a tea substitute.

The most attractive and flowery of the antipodean shrubs, grevilleas (*Proteaceae grevillea*) have become popular with gardeners all over the world, but they are Australian natives. They belong to the family of Proteaceae, which, because they are so variable in habitat, flower and foliage, are named after Proteus, the demi-god who could change his shape whenever he pleased. The genus is named after C.F. Greville, one of the founders of the Royal Horticultural Society. Grevilleas are attractive to birds, especially to honey-eaters, which find abundant sustenance among their flower-laden branches.

In the clay, sand and gravel soils of Albany, Western Australia, the bright yellow and red flowers of the pincushion hakea (*Hakea laurina*) are found growing in the bush from March to September. The hakea is a spectacular plant — it may grow to 7m, with drooping and weeping branches densely covered with blue-green leathery leaves. The tree was named after Baron von Hake, an 18th century professor of botany, and is valued for its perfume as much as for its beauty.

The green paperbark (*Melaleuca viridiflora*) grows to 18m with papery bark and elliptical leaves. It is found in Queensland, the Northern Territory and the north of Western Australia. Its cylindrical spiked pale green or pink flowers blossom for most of the year — the green paperbark is noted for these showy flowers and for its decorative peeling bark.

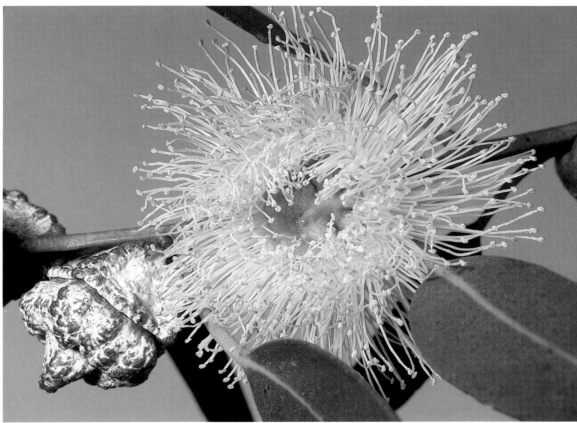

The tall smooth barked blue gum (*Eucalyptus globulus*) is the floral emblem of Tasmania and found in Tasmania and Victoria. The juvenile foliage of this stately tree is a blue-grey which deepens to a lush dark green — a perfect setting for the lovely white blossoms of the blue gum.

The bottlebrush is a distinctly Australian native tree. This is a willow bottlebrush (*Callistemon salignus*), which is found along creek banks in open forests on the coast of New South Wales and southern Queensland. A small tree, the willow bottlebrush grows to 9m, and has dense foliage which is pink when young, papery bark and narrow leaves. The branches of this evergreen weeping shrub are tipped with spectacular brush-like cream cylindrical flowers.

The colourful and sweet smelling scarlet banksia (*Banksia coccinea*) grows in the sandy heathlands of southwest Western Australia. The blossoms of the scarlet banksia are composed of hundreds of tiny flowers growing together in spikes or cones, and may reach 8cm in length and breadth. The banksia flowers in spring and its nectar-rich flowers have given it the popular name of honeysuckle, although it is also commonly known as bottlebrush. Banksias are named after Sir Joseph Banks, the English naturalist who first documented much of the Australian flora.

Banksia oblogifolia

The pretty emu bush (*Eremophila maculata*) flourishes in arid Australia and is sprinkled with tubular orange, red, yellow or pink flowers throughout the year. It is a very variable shrub, but usually grows to about 2m.

The lovely green-comb spider orchid (*Caladenia dilatata*) is a delicate flower, with long tapering petals and sepals. It is a temperate, deciduous terrestial orchid.

COLOURS

Newcomers to Australia are struck immediately by the light: the colour and the intensity. Long before they see their first kangaroo or utter their first oohs and aahs at the sight of a somnolent koala, the light has made its impression. It's clear, vivid, occasionally harsh. Even on a soft still city day — when banks of dove grey cloud shield the blue sky — the light is potent. In the country it's even stronger. No car exhaust fumes or factory fumes muddy the air; only bushfires or dust storms can choke the sky.

The badlands of Australia — the great deserts which cover nearly half the continent — can be giant, gently rolling, red sand dunes, flat gibber plains, sprawling white salt pans, burnt claypans . . . the colours are as varied as the country itself. The vastness creates a world with a colour of its own. The horizon is somewhere out there, lost in the purple of twilight and then the black of night. The rare rains can transform the deserts but in their usual dry state they create a palette of intangible life and colour. D.H. Lawrence in *The Kangaroo*, wrote: "The strange, as it were, invisible beauty of Australia, which is undeniably there but which seems to lurk just beyond the range of our white vision."

On the gibber plains, (gibber is an Aboriginal word meaning stone) the rocks shine with a coat of polish: a thin coating of iron oxide residue left by the desert winds. The seemingly lifeless desert can erupt in an ephemeral blaze of colour: the scarlet beauty of Sturt's Desert Pea flames after rain, transforming what was barren land. But even without the rain, the deserts are alive with a colour all their own. Ripples of sand dunes in the Simpson Desert create a light and dark stipple pattern in tan and orange or as the sun sets, purple and indigo.

But Ayers Rock steals the Outback colour carnival. In the false dawn, that lightening time before sunrise a pale light steals over the Rock, bathing it in a soft pink as the sky turns a pale blue. With the sun visible on the horizon the Rock begins to shimmer and glow. Gradually the face becomes an orange-red, the crevices and cracks creating varicose veins of black. In the heat of the day it seems red and ochre from close-up; bluer from a distance. Now it stands aloof and constant, waiting for the sunset that brings the colourful climax. The orange turns to brick red, to a harsh purple, to a soft deep mauve to black. All this is from the viewing points more than 1km from the Rock. But on the monolith itself the colours are vastly different: grey and lilac patterns can dance across the worn face; after the rain small silver lines sparkle in the creases. The Rock is a kaleidoscope.

The popular image of Australia is golden sand, blue skies, red desert. But the shimmering tracts of white saltpans and salt lakes are as big as some European states. Lake Eyre, the lowest point of the Australian continent is the biggest and best-known of these saltlands, covering 9300 square kilometres. A shimmering desolation, glittering and eerie. The arctic scene is out of place in this Dantesque inferno. In this uniformly salt-soaked world the colours change subtly: a flat white frost to a frothy pink-white where the delicate salt crystals rise in foam. While Lake Eyre is the king of the salt country, pockets of salt can be found across the wastelands — even in the far north separating the isolated settlement of Burketown from the Gulf of Carpentaria.

There can be a startling variety in these uninhabited tracts of Australia.

● Geikie Gorge, in the iron-rich Kimberley region of Western Australia has steep walls that sparkle like a jeweller's showcase of opal. The Outback Barrier Reef, Geikie Gorge has walls of orange, rust, pink, white, grey and black that seem to have been coloured by Rolf Harris — throwing paint around with abandon. Perhaps the most striking sight is on a clear windfree day when the colours on the walls are reflected in the water, seeming to pick up an even greater density of colour.

● Wave Rock, in the heart of Western Australia's wheatbelt is streaked with vertical stripes of red and orange and sandy grey, caused by water trickling down the face of the wave and picking up carbonates and iron hydroxide. A scar of white granite breaks the flow of colour in the wave.

● Compare the Wave with the waves . . . the Bungle Bungles. From the air they seem like a series of gently rolling brown waves. Virtually undiscovered — certainly by visitors and tourists — until 1983, the Bungle Bungles is a national park today. Remote, rugged and remarkable, the Bungle Bungles is a series of coloured whorls and loops. Like a vast line-up of fingerprints in shades of brown from near-ebony to a pale cream.

East of Perth near Hayden, this extraordinary rock formation looms out of the surrounding plain curving wave-like over itself. Wave Rock is an enormous sculptured wave more than 100m long and 15M tall on the northern side of Hayden Rock, which is about 2,700 million years old and part of one of the oldest land surfaces on Earth. The bands of red, ochre and grey across Wave Rock are caused by water trickling down the rock face leaving minerals which have stained its surface.

A sea of rustling grasses and a solitary ghost gum add a splatter of green to the orange of the Rock — the run-off from rain has produced a fertile belt of land around the base of Ayers Rock, where trees, shrubs and grasses flourish. Plants in the Red Centre struggle to survive and are equipped to survive long periods of drought. The desert is soaked by heavy rains only once or twice a decade, but in their wake the soil springs to life with the yellow, red and white of desert flowers. The weathered surface of Ayers Rock provides a natural guttering system for moisture to drip down and feed the plants sheltering beneath its grandeur — even the morning dew collects and runs down the rock to provide life maintaining moisture for these plants.

It is a giant leap from the centre of Australia to its coastline but the coast is such a contrast to the centre that inevitably it is the next colourful counterpoint. The red and orange of the centre fades alongside the remarkable blues and green waters of the great Barrier Reef. For 2000km along the Queensland coast, it is the mightiest coral reef system in the world. In reality the Reef is some 2500 individual reefs blocking the might of the Pacific Ocean from the coastline. The inside, protected waters are a dazzling blue, occasionally turning rich green. The vegetation on the reefs and islands is a lush tropical green and the beaches white to golden amber. A feast of colour.

But if the land and the sea form a colour band of their own, the corals of the reef represent an even more spectacular realm. There are about 400 species of coral polyps on the Reef — small, soft-bodied animals which die one by one to form a layer of limestone and ultimately a reef. They look like marine flowers, with a multi-variety of colour and shape. Brain coral (*Lobophyllia spp.*) with its patterned green clumps and orange coral (*Dendrophyllia spp.*) gain their colour from the living polyps. When they die only a white skeleton resides on the reef. There are soft corals such as the red organ pipe coral (*Tubipora musica*) and blue coral (*Heliopora coerulea*) which retain their colour after the polyps die.

So the Reef has beaches, sea, island vegetation, corals and . . . fish. The water is alive with nearly 2000 different species as well 10,000 species of sponge, more than 4000 species of mollusc, nearly 200 species of starfish, sea urchins and related species.

Too many colours, too many shapes to describe. But the beautiful butterfly fish (*Chaetodon spp.*) is characteristic of the reef: moving gracefully and airily among the coral. The reef crab (*Metopograpsus spp.*) stands out among the shellfish with its bright blue shell and tonal hues sparkling like an underwater opal. The Reef is alive with a colour all its own.

It's a large leap from the Reef in the tropics to the Australian Alps. But the diversity of Australia and its colours is highlighted in the abrupt transition to the alpine part of the Great Dividing Range. Although officially called Alps, Australia's mountain region reaches a high point of only 2228metres (Mt Kosciusko) — small by global standards and miniscule in comparison with Mt Everest (8841metres). The scenery in our Alps, because of its lower altitudes

Summer dust storms sweep over Melbourne in the summer of 1982–83. Their blanketing umbrella cast a pall over the Victorian capital. Major dust storms are a product of drought and its savage eroding quality.

changes dramatically with the seasons. In winter 6000-7000 square kilometres of high country is covered with thick, usually ski-able snow. The first snows generally fall round June, lasting through to September, even October. In the shadows and cracks hidden from the winter sun, algae shimmer through the thin snow cover. Some red-pigmented species create a blood-stained effect. But the flora which thrives in the harsh conditions are the snow gums (*Eucalyptus pauciflora*). No Norwegian spruces or Canadian firs in these mountains: the distinctively Australian look comes from the gums with their tortured shapes growing to a height of eight metres. The smooth white bark of the gum is streaked and mottled with russet, green, even gold bands. Their colourful display is often matched by a blanket of Alpine paper daisies (*Helipterum albicans*), their icy green stems supporting a yolk yellow heart and familiar white petals.

The deserts, the Reef, the coast, the Alps. They all have distinctive energy, distinctive colourings. So too, does the Bush, that vast expanse of Australia which comes in so many shades and hues. The vegetation has an enormous capacity for regeneration after fire — a permanent threat in Australia's hot, dry climate. This has been a major feature in shaping, and colouring, the forests and bushland. The country's most characteristic plant is the eucalypt; its leaves are full of flammable oils which, ironically, protect the tree in a fire. The leaves flame and flare fiercely but briefly. Generally the fire is so quick, with the oil-loaded leaves fuelling the flames, that it passes through rapidly, leaving the tree itself charred and battered but not destroyed. Eucalypts have evolved into hundreds of species but there are common characteristics: the trunks are slender and light in colour, the foliage is silver through to olive green, casting little shadow. This gives the Australian bush its open, light quality.

Australia is a natural light gallery. But man has played his part, sometimes well, sometimes awkwardly. The first buildings of sandstone gave the newly-urban Australia a soft warm feeling; later buildings were hastily thrown-up concrete slabs. The roofs of Sydney are instantly recognisable when a jumbo jet breaks through a thin cover of coastal cloud and swoops down on the city: row after row of red tiles stare back at the passengers. These are permanent colours, welded to the framework of the island continent.

Then there are the ephemeral colours, brilliant and memorable for those lucky enough to capture them: fireworks over Sydney Harbour, the razzle and dazzle of Melbourne's annual Moomba Festival, the reflection of lights shining on the halyards of the Sydney-Hobart Fleet as it sits wearily at anchor in the Derwent.

But above all the nuances and shades of Australia sits the umbrella: that unique sky. That blue which taunts description and colours every view of the continent.

A timeless scene in the metallic hues of sunset —
rich copper sands and sky frame the molten silver
waters of an unusually serene Southern Ocean.
This is William Bay National Park, west of Albany in
Western Australia. The narrow sandy beaches and
low headlands of the park are popular fishing spots
and beyond the coastal stretches lie dunes dotted
with stunted peppermint trees and a small
karri forest.

A tranquil beach scene on the coast of New South
Wales — a platinum sea washes the darkening
sands while a family watches the evening draw on.

The beautiful mist-shrouded countryside of New South Wales is the perfect setting for Mt Seaview Lodge, west of Wauchope on the Oxley Highway. Set on the banks of the magnificent Hastings River, in a magical valley speckled with deep swimming holes, Mt Seaview Lodge offers a wide choice of outdoor activities: horse-riding, gold panning, bush exploring.

Stark, uniformed trees in an open stand on the Pacific Highway near Kempsey, provide a quiet retreat for a lone Fresian.

Byron Bay is the surfing mecca of New South Wales and Watego's Beach is one of its many popular surfing destinations. As the sun leaves the beach and the sea a tranquil timelessness descends over this lovely and most easterly point of Australia. Byron is loved by surfers from all over the world because of its beaches which face different directions — whether there's a nor'easterly or a southerly, there is always a swell at Byron Bay. Scuba divers also flock to the area, where Australia's first marine sanctuary protects hard and soft corals and a great variety of marine life.

The Duracks and other early settlers of the eastern Kimberley, having travelled across the dry plains of the Northern Territory, would have welcomed the deep blue waters of Lake Argyle for their thirsty cattle. They fought drought and flood to survive in this harsh region from the mid-1880s. In 1972 the racing waters of the Ord River were dammed to form the serene indigo of Lake Argyle, a lake nine times the volume of Sydney Harbour. Fruit, vegetables, sorghum and sunflowers now thrive in this once hazardous environment.

These golden stalks of budding wheat are a common sight in Australia as summer approaches and the wheat ripens ready for the annual harvest. Wheat is one of Australia's most important primary industries and since about the 1870s Australia has been a regular wheat exporting nation. The first wheat grown in Australia was sown by convicts on the site of Sydney's Botanic Gardens. By 1895, 1.4 million hectares were under wheat in Australia. In 1968-69 nearly 10.8 million hectares were planted throughout the country.

The rich red, bronze and gold reflections of the walls of Geikie Gorge are marbled by the afternoon sun across the Fitzroy River.

The sea and tides have played a central role in the history of Point Samson, which is found in the famous Pilbara region of Western Australia, southwest of Port Hedland. Walter Padbury first settled this district, and named the point after his friend Michael Samson who accompanied him on his travels in the area in 1863. Point Samson eventually became an important port, and by 1910 it was the major port for the region, exporting asbestos from Wittenoom until 1968 and copper and wool. Since 1976 Point Samson has been a much quieter town, supported by its fishing industry and tourism.

This peaceful Surfers Paradise sunrise belies the
fact that Surfers Paradise is one of Australia's fastest
growing tourist areas. Within a few hours the beach
will be bursting with sun-seekers and the tranquil
roses and soft golds of the dawn will be
transformed into the daytime dazzling blue and
shimmering yellow of the Pacific Ocean and
its beaches.

The drama of an Australian sunset — dark looming shadows beckon the night while the last deep yellows of the daylight world slip quietly into the west.

The soft pinks, ivories and yellows of coral buds and branches blossom on an outer reef of Heron Island at low tide. These corals are reef builders, growing very rapidly in thick profusion in a highly co-ordinated manner. From October to December, soon after a full moon, the darkness of the night triggers the release of a milky sea of eggs, sperm and larvae, as the corals undergo their annual reproduction ritual.

The ethereal calm of two blues, where the glittering turquoise of the Indian Ocean meets the soft jacaranda of the sky, makes a striking contrast to the dangerous shores of much of the coastline of Western Australia, where fierce seas and rugged cliffs have destroyed hundreds of ships.

The vibrant red of coral woven through the dark
waters of the Pacific makes a striking web of colour
on the Great Barrier Reef. The corals are the
dominant creatures of the Reef — about 350
species of coral are found in the 2,300km of reef,
which runs along the coastal shelf of north
eastern Australia.

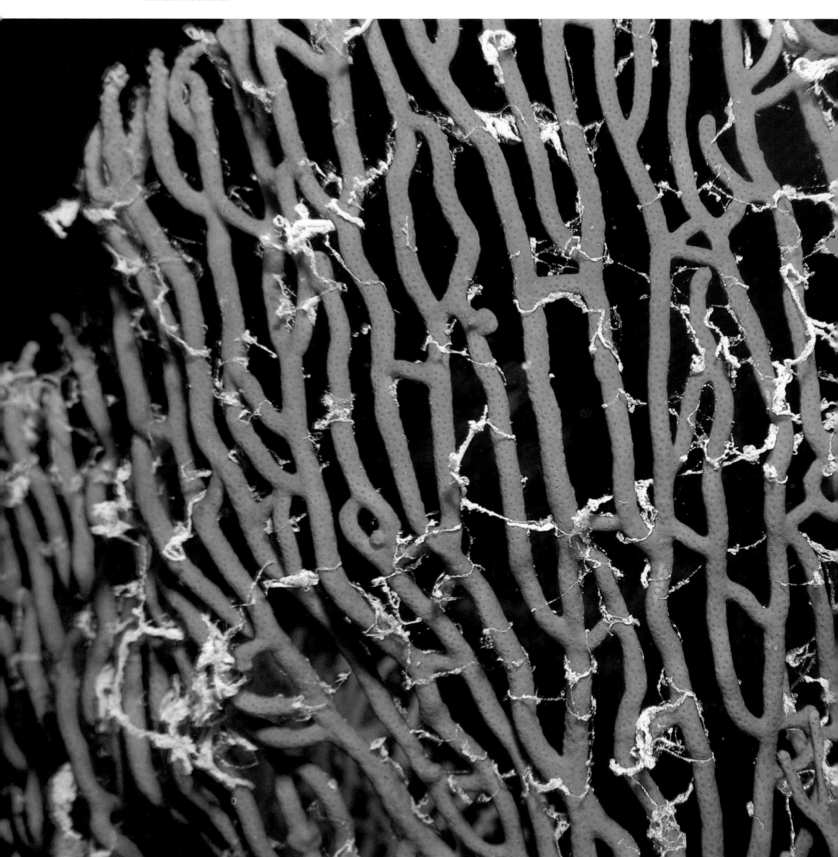

The sculptured white spines of the Murex pecten blend perfectly with the palest of creamy yellow sands that line the shores of the Barrier Reef. The Barrier Reef is a shell lover's paradise — many of the islands and reefs are protected, so shells survive in abundance. Despite its fierce spikes, this shell is a mild creature compared with some of the reef shells — the beautiful cone shell, a carnivorous hunter, can be extremely venomous to humans.

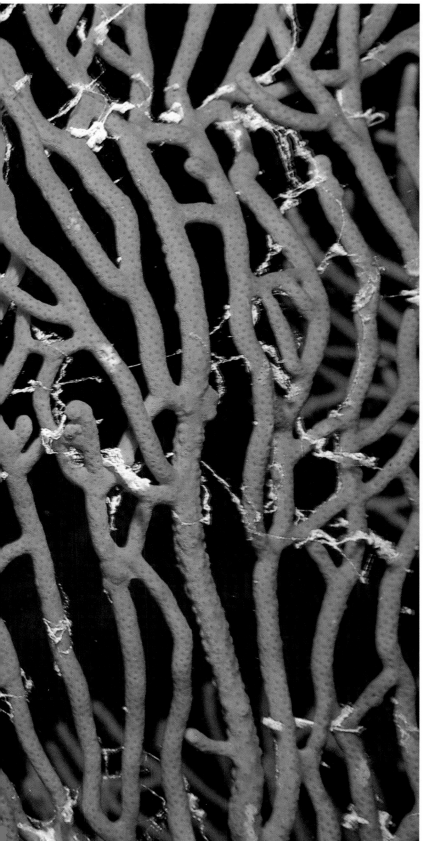

The delicate hues of these corals glow beneath the waters of the Pacific Ocean, topped by the silver shimmer of a school of reef fish. These are brain corals, hard corals named for their convoluted brain-like surface. The hard corals are associated with the construction of the reef; while the soft corals can be seen as the decorators of the reef. The hard corals are the builders, forming the structure of the reef.

The faded colours of central Australia indicate the scarcity of water and the cruelty of the sun in the heart of the island continent. This solitary ruin of a stone cottage serves as a reminder of the battling attempts of European man to settle this area.

The tangled rainforest of Fraser Island is a splash of green on the largest sand island in the world. Fraser Island is also the largest island off Queensland's coast, a beautiful tropical paradise of endless beaches, rainforest jungle, freshwater lakes and swamps. Fraser Island covers 1,550sq km and supports several popular resorts — it is a sunlover's paradise, a fisherman's playground and a bird enthusiast's sanctuary as its wide variety of vegetation attracts more than 240 species of birds. Fraser Island was sighted by Captain Cook in 1770 but, not realizing it was an island, he did not name it. The island was eventually named after Captain James Fraser, who was killed by Aborigines after his ship the *Stirling Castle* was wrecked on its shores.

The fantastic colours of the Pilbara in northern Western Australia are admired by painters all over Australia. The rich copper soil brushed by tussocks of pale golden hummock grass reaches into the eternity of a blazing blue sky. The region is the home of Hamersley iron and other mineral deposits found in rugged ranges of ancient origin and spectacular beauty. The abundant ore deposits of the Pilbara contribute to the dramatic colouring of the rocks and soils of this untamed country.

Windswept sand and windswept cloud echo each other across the silence of the Pinnacles Desert in Western Australia, 250km north of Perth. The soft yellow of this sandy desert sweeps to the Indian Ocean, an undisturbed sea of quartz sand rippled by the wind. The desert is named after the strange limestone formations that loom up out of the sands in pillars, knobs and spires, some as thin as a little finger and others as large as the stones of Stonehenge.

The colours of central Australia are contained in its burning orange wind-ridged sands and grey-green spinifex grasses, which lie beneath a vast blue domed sky — empty earth, empty sky. The vivid blue of the sky pales to a washed-out blue, faded by the intense heat of the desert sun. And man, even in this remote corner, has left his mark. The deserts receive less than 250 millimetres of annual rainfall, so the occasional clouded sky is all that offers relief from the heat in the flat infinity of red. Deserts cover almost half of Australia — these powerful landscapes have fixed a hold on the national consciousness and have fascinated Australian writers and painters.

Late afternoon in Geikie Gorge — the magnificent colours of the limestone walls of the gorge are washed across the mirror of the Fitzroy River. This beautiful gorge lies in the Kimberley and has its origins over 350 million years ago in an ancient limestone reef. The walls are whitewashed each summer during the Big Wet, when the waters of the 200m wide Fitzroy River rise up to 16m leaving a band of dazzling white across the warm orange walls.

The Australian Boab can live for hundreds of years and grows up to 18 m tall and 2 m wide. This boab is near Windjana Gorge in the Kimberleys, its silver grey trunk shimmering in the sun and its spindly arms stretching into the deep blue sky. The boab, or bottle tree, grows on stony hills and sandy plains in northern Western Australia. The wood of the boab yields an edible jelly and the young roots and seeds were once the favoured food of the local Aborigines — today the trunk and leaves of the boab are still used as emergency fodder for livestock during droughts.

The red-leaved palm (*Livistona Mariae*) is unique to Palm Valley, in Finke Gorge National Park, central Australia. Only about 700 of these palms survive, reminders of the moist and fertile past of inland Australia, and are among the oldest plants in the world. This species of cabbage-tree palm is a stately plant, reaching a height of 15m, with large fan-like leaves.

The dazzling two-toned sandstone of the Hermannsburg rock wall looms over the parched red claypan, sand and spinifex of Rainbow Valley. After the annual rains which fall in August and September this arid sandy plain becomes an oasis of purple and yellow wildflowers. The colours of the valley were formed by rainwater and underground water leaching iron oxide from deep in the rock, colouring the upper areas red and hardening them — the same water action bleached the lower areas of rock, which resulted in the distinctive brick red and cream stripes of the Hermannsburg cliff formation.

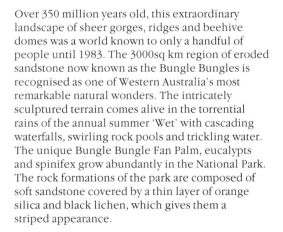

Over 350 million years old, this extraordinary landscape of sheer gorges, ridges and beehive domes was a world known to only a handful of people until 1983. The 3000sq km region of eroded sandstone now known as the Bungle Bungles is recognised as one of Western Australia's most remarkable natural wonders. The intricately sculptured terrain comes alive in the torrential rains of the annual summer 'Wet' with cascading waterfalls, swirling rock pools and trickling water. The unique Bungle Bungle Fan Palm, eucalypts and spinifex grow abundantly in the National Park. The rock formations of the park are composed of soft sandstone covered by a thin layer of orange silica and black lichen, which gives them a striped appearance.

The evening purple mingles with the lights as the Opera House comes alive. The $100 million Opera House has a 1700-seat main hall, a 1550-seat auditorium, an intimate theatre, several speciality halls and superb restaurants.

The Sydney Harbour Bridge was opened on 19 March, 1932 after nine years construction. The largest arch bridge in the world it is 134m from sea level to the top of its famous arch. The main span of the bridge reaches 503m from the Rocks to Milson's Point. The arching grandeur of this beautiful bridge contains 52,000 tons of steel.

That magical moment that will live for a
lifetime. . .the First Fleet re-enactment ships arrive
in Sydney Harbour on Australia Day, 1988, a
harbour scene like nowhere else in the world!

193

Willoura Station, a 40,400ha merino stud at
Conargo, near Deniliquin, is the setting for an
essentially Australian scene. A horse, that
distinctive Australian sky and the sunburnt land.

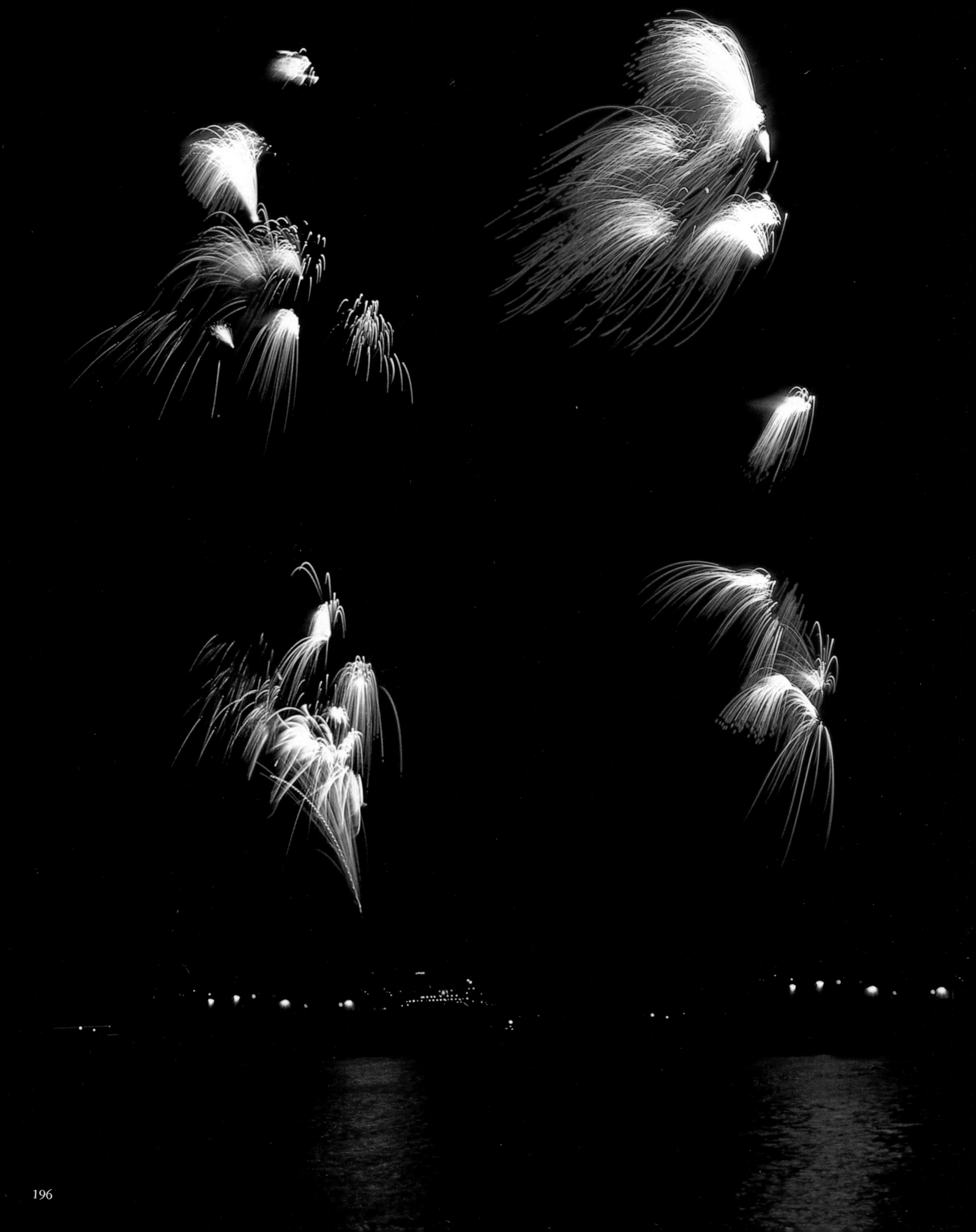

Photo Credits

The publishers acknowledge the following for permission to reproduce their photographs:

Front cover:	Mark Lang, Wildlight
Page 2:	Bruno Jean Grasswill
Page 7:	Bruno Jean Grasswill
Page 9:	Bruno Jean Grasswill
Page 11:	Australian Tourist Commission
Page 14:	Tom and Pam Gardner/A.N.T. Photo Library
Page 16:	M. Lees/ Australian Picture Library
Page 17:	(Top) Bruno Jean Grasswill
	(Middle) J. Carnemolla/Australian Picture Library
	(Bottom) Bruno Jean Grasswill
Page 18/19:	Wildlight, Grenville Turner
Page 20/21:	(Top) Tony Feder/Impressions
	(Bottom Left) Paul Steel/Stock Photos
	(Bottom Right) Bill Bachman/Stock Photos
Page 23:	Australian Tourist Commission
Page 24/25:	(Top) C. Copeland/Australian Picture Library
	(Bottom) C. Copeland/Australian Picture Library
Page 26:	Australian Tourist Commission
Page 27:	Stock Photos
Page 28/29:	R. Garvey/Australian Picture Library
Page 30:	Australian Tourist Commission
Page 31:	Wildlight, Phillip Quirk
Page 32:	(Top) Australian Tourist Commission
	(Bottom) Australian Tourist Commission
Page 33:	Bill Bachman/Stock Photos
Page 34:	Australian Tourist Commission
Page 35:	(Top) Australian Tourist Commission
	(Middle) Australian Tourist Commission
	(Bottom) Australian Tourist Commission
Page 36/37:	(Top) Silent Picture Show Pty Ltd, Stuart Owen Fox
	(Bottom) Australian Tourist Commission
Page 38/39:	Australian Tourist Commission
Page 40:	(Top) Stuart Owen Fox
	(Bottom) Stuart Owen Fox
Page 41:	(Top) Australian Tourist Commission
	(Bottom) J.B. Anderson
Page 42:	Paul Steel/Stock Photos
Page 43:	Australian Tourist Commission
Page 44:	(Top) Australian Tourist Commission
	(Bottom) Australian Tourist Commission
Page 45:	Australian Tourist Commission
Page 46/47:	Australian Tourist Commission
Page 48:	(Top) Australian Tourist Commission
	(Bottom) David Cimino/Stock Photos
Page 49:	Phillip Hayson/Stock Photos
Page 50:	J. Barry Anderson
Page 51:	J. Barry Anderson
Page 52:	(Top) Australian Tourist Commission
	(Bottom) Australian Tourist Commission
Page 53:	(Top) Australian Tourist Commission
	(Bottom) Australian Tourist Commission
Page 54:	Australian Tourist Commission
Page 55:	Dallas & John Heaton/Australian Picture Library
Page 56:	Australian Tourist Commission
Page 57:	Bill Bachman/Stock Photos
Page 58:	(Top) Australian Tourist Commission
	(Bottom) Bill Bachman/Stock Photos
Page 59:	Australian Tourist Commission
Page 60:	Australian Tourist Commission
Page 60/61:	(Top) J. Barry Anderson
	(Bottom) Australian Tourist Commission
Page 62:	Bill Bachman/Stock Photos
Page 63:	(Top) J. Barry Anderson
	(Bottom) Australian Tourist Commission
Page 65:	Australian Tourist Commission
Page 68:	Australian Tourist Commission
Page 69:	Wildlight, Oliver Strewe
Page 72/73:	(Top) Wildlight, Grenville Turner
Page 72:	(Bottom) Australian Tourist Commission
Page 73:	(Bottom) Australian Tourist Commission
Page 74:	John Carnemolla/Australian Picture Library
Page 75:	Australian Tourist Commission
Page 76:	Wildlight, Grenville Turner
Page 77:	Australian Tourist Commission
Page 78:	(Top) Bill Bachman/Stock Photos
	(Bottom) Australian Tourist Commission
Page 79:	Australian Tourist Commission
Page 80:	Wildlight, Carolyn Johns
Page 81:	Australian Tourist Commission
Page 82:	Australian Tourist Commission
Page 83:	Australian Tourist Commission
Page 84/85:	Australian Tourist Commission
Page 86/87:	(Top) Wildlight, Grenville Turner
	(Bottom) Australian Tourist Commission
Page 88/89:	Bill Bachman/Stock Photos
Page 90:	John Carnemolla/Stock Photos
Page 91:	Tony Martorano/Stock Photos
Page 92:	Australian Tourist Commission
Page 93:	Australian Tourist Commission
Page 94:	Australian Tourist Commission
Page 95:	Australian Tourist Commission
Page 96:	(Top) Bruno Jean Grasswill
Page 96/97:	Bruno Jean Grasswill
Page 97:	(Top) Bruno Jean Grasswill
Page 98:	Australian Tourist Commission
Page 99:	(Top) Australian Tourist Commission
	(Bottom) Australian Tourist Commission, Stuart Owen Fox
Page 100/101:	Stuart Owen Fox
Page 102:	(Top) Australian Tourist Commission
	(Middle) Australian Tourist Commission
	(Bottom) J. Carnemolla/ Australian Picture Library
Page 103:	John Carnemolla/Australian Picture Library
Page 104:	Tony Feder/Impressions
Page 105:	John Carnemolla/Australian Picture Library
Page 106:	(Top) Australian Tourist Commission
	(Bottom) Australian Tourist Commission
Page 107:	Stuart Owen Fox
Page 108:	Australian Tourist Commission
Page 109:	(Top) Australian Tourist Commission
	(Bottom) Australian Tourist Commission
Page 111:	Bruno Jean Grasswill
Page 112:	Ralph and Daphne Keller/A.N.T. Photo Library
Page 115:	Dave Watts/A.N.T. Photo Library
Page 116:	Bruno Jean Grasswill
Page 117:	M.Provic/A.N.T. Photo Library
Page 118:	Otto Rogge/A.N.T. Photo Library
Page 119:	(Top) Dave Watts/A.N.T. Photo Library
	(Bottom) Otto Rogge/A.N.T. Photo Library
Page 120:	Dave Watts/A.N.T. Photo Library
Page 121:	G.B. Baker/A.N.T. Photo Library
Page 122:	G. & R. Wilson/A.N.T. Photo Library
Page 123:	C. & S. Pollitt/A.N.T. Photo Library
Page 124:	Ralph & Daphne Keller/A.N.T. Photo Library
Page 125:	Ken Griffiths/A.N.T. Photo Library
Page 126:	Wildlight, Carolyn Johns
Page 127:	Australian Tourist Commission, Stuart Owen Fox
Page 128:	(Bottom) J. Frazier/A.N.T. Photo Library
Page 128/129:	John Cann/A.N.T. Photo Library
Page 129:	(Middle) M.J. Tyler/A.N.T. Photo Library
	(Bottom) M. Davies/A.N.T. Photo Library
Page 130:	A. Dennis/A.N.T. Photo Library
Page 131:	J. Weigel/A.N.T. Photo Library
Page 132:	Otto Rogge/A.N.T. Photo Library
Page 133:	G.E. Schmida/A.N.T. Photo Library

Page 134:	G.E. Schmida/A.N.T. Photo Library	Page 192:	John Carnemolla/Australian Picture Library
Page 135:	G.E. Schmida/A.N.T. Photo Library	Page 193:	Bruno Jean Grasswill
Page 136:	G. Anderson/A.N.T. Photo Library	Page 194/195:	Australian Tourist Commission
Page 137:	B.G. Thomson/A.N.T. Photo Library	Page 196/197:	Bruno Jean Grasswill
Page 138:	Ken Griffiths/A.N.T. Photo Library	Page 200:	D. Bishop/A.N.T. Photo Library
Page 139:	D. Clyne/A.N.T. Photo Library		
Page 140:	James Rule/A.N.T. Photo Library		
Page 141:	Freddy Mercay/A.N.T. Photo Library		
Page 142:	Otto Rogge/A.N.T. Photo Library		
Page 143:	Denis & Theresa O'Byrne/A.N.T. Photo Library		
Page 144/145:	D. Rogge/A.N.T. Photo Library		
Page 146:	G. Wood/A.N.T. Photo Library		
Page 147:	Otto Rogge/A.N.T. Photo Library		
Page 148:	Otto Rogge/A.N.T. Photo Library		
Page 149:	Ted Hutchinson/A.N.T. Photo Library		
Page 150:	Frank Park/A.N.T. Photo Library		
Page 151:	Jan Taylor/A.N.T. Photo Library		
Page 152:	(Top) Otto Rogge/A.N.T. Photo Library		
	(Bottom) Australian Picture Library		
Page 153:	(Top left) G. Cheers/A.N.T. Photo Library		
	(Top right) G. Cheers/A.N.T. Photo Library		
	(Bottom) Otto Rogge/A.N.T. Photo Library		
Page 154:	G. & B. Cheers/A.N.T. Photo Library		
Page 155:	G.A. Wood/A.N.T. Photo Library		
Page 156:	Keith Williams/A.N.T. Photo Library		
Page 157:	I.R. McCann/A.N.T. Photo Library		
Page 158:	Ralph & Daphne Keller/A.N.T. Photo Library		
Page 159:	Fritz Prenzel/Australian Picture Library		
Page 160:	Otto Rogge/A.N.T. Photo Library		
Page 161:	Otto Rogge/A.N.T. Photo Library		
Page 163:	Bruno Jean Grasswill		
Page 164:	Bruno Jean Grasswill		
Page 165:	Australian Tourist Commission		
Page 166:	Bill Bachman/Stock Photos		
Page 168:	Australian Tourist Commission		
Page 169:	Australian Tourist Commission		
Page 170:	(Top) The Silent Picture Show Pty Ltd, Stuart Owen Fox		
	(Middle) The Silent Picture Show Pty Ltd, Stuart Owen Fox		
	(Bottom) The Silent Picture Show Pty Ltd, Stuart Owen Fox		
Page 172:	Bruno Jean Grasswill		
Page 173:	(Top) Australian Tourist Commission		
	(Bottom) Australian Tourist Commission		
Page 174:	(Top) Bill Bachman/Stock Photos		
	(Bottom) Bill Bachman/Stock Photos		
Page 175:	Australian Tourist Commission		
Page 176:	(Top) Bruno Jean Grasswill		
	(Bottom) Australian Tourist Commission		
Page 177:	Bruno Jean Grasswill		
Page 178:	Bill Bachman/Stock Photos		
Page 179:	Australian Tourist Commission		
Page 180:	Australian Tourist Commission		
Page 181:	(Top) Australian Tourist Commission		
	(Middle) Australian Tourist Commission		
	(Bottom) Australian Tourist Commission		
Page 182:	Australian Tourist Commission		
Page 183:	Australian Tourist Commission		
Page 184:	(Left) Bill Bachman/Stock Photos		
	(Right) Bill Bachman/Stock Photos		
Page 185:	Wildlight, Grenville Turner		
Page 186:	Wildlight, Carolyn Johns		
Page 187:	(Top) Bill Bachman/Stock Photos		
	(Bottom) Grant Dixon/A.N.T. Photo Library		
Page 188:	Wildlight, Carolyn Johns		
Page 189:	(Top) Australian Tourist Commission		
	(Bottom) Australian Tourist Commission		
Page 190:	Bruno Jean Grasswill		
Page 191:	Bruno Jean Grasswill		

Acknowledgements

The publishers wish to give special thanks to the following for their assistance in the production of this book:

The Surf Life Saving Association of Australia
Northern Territory Government Tourist Bureau
Central Mapping Authority of New South Wales
Tourism Commission of New South Wales
Western Australian Tourist Centre
South Australian Bicentennial Commission
Australian Stockman's Hall of Fame
Herbarium, Royal Botanic Gardens, Sydney
Paul, Taronga Zoo
Fiona Campbell, John Flynn Centre, Cloncurry
Michael Hill
Stuart Owen Fox, The Silent Picture Show Pty Ltd
Maritime Services Board of New South Wales
Royal Australian Navy
Commonwealth Department of Transport and Communications
David Seabrook, Hotel Albert, Monto
Viv Morgan, Monto
Elders Pastoral — Brisbane, Sydney, Hay, Deniliquin, Katherine, Alice Springs and Darwin offices
Mr Lamb, Willoura Station
Damien Miller, Hamilton Downs
Fay and Stan, Kynuna Post Office
Rod Rolfe, Yorkshire Downs
Mr and Mrs Evatt, Winton
Roger Green, Growth Equities Mutual Ltd
Barbara Haines, Women's Weekly
Stewart West, Parliament House, Canberra
Darling Harbour Authority

The frilled lizard (*Chlamydosaurus kingii*).